TRUDY DAVIDSON

From Concept to Creation: Your Ultimate Guide To Writing Picture Books And Self Publishing

Copyright © 2024 by Trudy Davidson

All rights reserved. No part of this publication may be reproduced, stored or transmitted in any form or by any means, electronic, mechanical, photocopying, recording, scanning, or otherwise without written permission from the publisher. It is illegal to copy this book, post it to a website, or distribute it by any other means without permission.

Trudy Davidson asserts the moral right to be identified as the author of this work.

Trudy Davidson has no responsibility for the persistence or accuracy of URLs for external or third-party Internet Websites referred to in this publication and does not guarantee that any content on such Websites is, or will remain, accurate or appropriate.

Designations used by companies to distinguish their products are often claimed as trademarks. All brand names and product names used in this book and on its cover are trade names, service marks, trademarks and registered trademarks of their respective owners. The publishers and the book are not associated with any product or vendor mentioned in this book. None of the companies referenced within the book have endorsed the book.

First edition

ISBN: 9781739121761

This book was professionally typeset on Reedsy. Find out more at reedsy.com

This book is dedicated to aspiring authors everywhere—may your journey be filled with creativity, perseverance, and joy. Keep believing in your stories; they can inspire children and delight readers of all ages.

Contents

Preface	x
How did it begin for me?	x
Who am I?	xiii
1 Picture Book Definition and Key Areas	1
Engaging Stories with Illustrations	1
A Summary of Picture Book Essentials	2
Simplicity and Succinctness	2
Age-appropriate Language	2
Message, Morals, and Themes	3
Read-Aloud Appeal	3
Layout and Format	4
Emphasis on Strong Visuals	4
Appealing Characters	5
2 Identify your audience	6
Deciding the Right Age Group for Your Picture Book	6
How Long Should a Picture Book Be?	8
Standard Picture Book Length	8
Transitioning to Chapter Books	9
Tailoring Stories from Ages 2 to 8	9
The Role and Significance of Illustrations in Picture Books	10
Understanding Picture Book Buyers Through Statistics	10

Questions to Consider When Defining Your Audience	11
Chapter Summary	12
3 Choose a message, a moral, or a theme	13
Exploring Themes, Messages and Morals in Picture Books	13
What is a Theme?	13
What is a Message?	14
What is a Moral?	14
Examples of Themes, Messages and Morals in My Picture Books	15
Drawing from Personal Experiences	18
Exploring Other Options and Considerations	18
Chapter Summary	20
4 The Ideas	21
Techniques to Spark Your Storytelling Journey	21
Lists to Generate Ideas for Your Picture Book	21
Mind Maps for Visualising Your Message, Moral, or Theme for Your Picture Book	22
Drawing from Personal Experience	24
Stories Inspired by My Own Experience	24
Character Inspiration from Personal Experiences	25
Observation for Inspiration	26
Brainstorming with Others	27
Creating Unforgettable Characters for Children	27
What Adults Look for in Children's Books	28
Relax and Spark Creativity	28
Chapter Summary	30
5 Create a compelling story	31
Developing a Simple and Engaging Plot	31
Creating Characters for Book Series Potential	32

Examples of Themes in My Picture Books	32
Embracing Happy Endings in Picture Books	34
Aligning Plot Complexity with Your Target Age Group in Picture Books	35
Reading Your Draft to Your Target Audience	36
Chapter Summary	36
6 Layout And Format	37
Choosing the Right Layout and Format for Your Picture Book	37
Creating Meaningful Dedications in Your Picture Book	38
A Pictorial Guide to a 32-Page Picture Book	39
Key Picture Book Sections Explained	39
Chapter Summary	45
7 Copyright	46
Copyright Information	46
A Useful Article on Copyright	48
Use the Copyright Symbol	48
Placement of Copyright Information in Your Book	48
Chapter Summary	49
8 Book Size (Trim Size)	50
Choosing the Right Trim Size for Your Picture Book	50
The Importance of Book Size	51
Print Cost Online Calculator	53
Chapter Summary	54
9 The Rough Draft	55
Choosing Your Writing Style	55
Types of Rhyme in Writing	55
End Rhyme	56

Internal Rhyme	56
Perfect Rhyme (or Exact Rhyme)	56
Slant Rhyme (or Near Rhyme)	56
Eye Rhyme	57
Rich Rhyme	57
Identical Rhyme	57
Masculine Rhyme	57
Feminine Rhyme	58
Monorhyme	58
Chain Rhyme	59
Past and Present Tense	59
First Person or Third Person	61
Crafting Your Picture Book with Style and Audience in Mind	64
Gathering Feedback	65
Overcoming Writer's Block	66
Chapter Summary	67
10 Self-Editing	68
Editing Your Draft to Refine Your Final Version	68
Enhancing Your Manuscript with Outside Perspectives	70
Chapter Summary	71
11 Professional Editing	72
Hiring a Professional Editor	72
Development Editing	73
Line Editing	73
Content Editing	74
Copy Editing	75
Ensuring Your Editor has a Clear Understanding of Your Book	75
The Benefits of Hiring a Professional Editor for Your Manuscript	76

Finding Editors Websites to Begin Your Search	77
Chapter Summary	78
12 Proofreading	79
Understanding the Role of a Proofreader in Document Preparation	79
Areas Covered by a Proofreader in Document Review	80
Websites to Begin Your Proofreader Search	81
Chapter Summary	82
13 Choosing A Title	83
Tips for Choosing a Title for Your Picture Book	83
Using Keywords Effectively in Your Book Title	84
Guidelines for Creating a Picture Book Title	85
Feedback on your Book Title Idea	86
Chapter Summary	87
14 Illustrations	88
Finding the Right Illustrator for Your Picture Book	88
Starting Your Search for an Illustrator	89
Things to Consider When Choose an Illustrator	90
Illustration Costs to Consider	92
Payment Structures for Illustrators	93
Illustration Approval Process	94
Text Placement in Illustrations	95
Managing Text Placement in Your Picture Book	96
Communicating Your Vision to the Illustrator	97
Example of Notes to the Illustrator	98
Trimming and Bleed Allowances in Book Publishing	104
Provide the ISBN and Barcode to Your Illustrator	105
Understanding the Gutter	105
Inform the Illustrator of Any Dedications	106

Chapter Summary	106
15 The Cover	107
DIY vs. Hiring a Professional	107
Guiding Your Front Cover Design	108
Utilising Amazon to Explore Picture Book Styles	109
Incorporating Sketches into the Illustration Process	111
Designing a Front Cover Wrap-around Illustration	112
Crafting an Engaging Picture Book Cover	112
Engaging Your Audience in Cover Design	114
Crafting a Compelling Back Cover for Your Picture Book	115
Finalising Your Book Cover	117
Securing Your Completed Book	118
Chapter Summary	119
16 ISBN and Bar Codes	120
What is an ISBN?	120
What is a Barcode?	122
An example of an ISBN and Barcode	122
Understanding ISBN and Barcode Costs for Self-Publishing	123
Understanding the Importance of ISBNs in Publishing	123
Managing ISBNs and Barcodes for Your Books	124
Considerations of Choosing Between Free and Purchased ISBNs	125
Chapter Summary	126
17 Comparing Online Retailers	127
A Guide to Choosing the Right Online Platform	127
Guidelines for Uploading Books on IngramSpark	130
What is the Trim Size?	130
Accounting for Bleed	131

Page Formatting	131
Benefits of Uploading eBook and Print Book Simultaneously	132
Chapter Summary	133
18 Uploading Your Files for a Printed Book	134
Setting Up Your Account	135
Uploading Your Book A Step-by-Step Guide	135
After Uploading Your Book	145
Chapter Summary	147
19 Uploading your files (e-book)	148
Choosing Different Platforms for eBooks and Printed Books	148
Exploring eBooks for Picture Books	149
Setting Up Your Account	150
Uploading Your Book A Step-by-Step Guide	150
Category Search Assistance	152
Chapter Summary	152
20 Keywords	153
The Importance of Keywords for Your Book	153
A Valuable Resource for Keywords and Competitive Insights	154
Chapter Summary	155
21 Author Central	156
The Benefits of Joining Amazon Author Central	156
Creating Your Amazon Author Central Account	156
Chapter Summary	159
22 Marketing	160
From Manuscript to Market	160
Social Media Platforms	161
Planning a Book Launch Marketing Campaign	163

Launch Team	164
How to Build a Launch Team	165
Managing the Launch Team	166
KDP Select and Verified Reviews	168
Launch Day	169
Setting Posts to Public	169
Clean Links And Why They Are Important	170
Join Social Media Groups	171
Creating a Website for Your Book	172
Paying For Advertising	174
Key Dates Throughout The Year	174
Share Received Reviews	175
Attend Promotional Events	175
Consider School Visits	176
Chapter Summary	178
23 Book Awards	179
Benefits of Winning Book Awards	179
Enhancing Your Visibility with Book Awards	180
Marketing Opportunities Through Book Awards	180
Submission Fees and Discounts for Book Awards	180
Displaying Your Winning Seal	181
Chapter Summary	181
24 Legal Deposit Regulations	182
Understanding Legal Deposit in the United Kingdom	182
Mailing Address for Legal Deposit	182
The Five Main UK Libraries	183
Automatic Right of the British Library	184
Legal Deposit Benefits	184
Chapter Summary	185
25 Plush (Soft) Toys	186
Expanding Into Merchandise	186

Toy Safety Regulations	187
Testing	188
Creating a Technical File	189
Exploring Manufacturing Options	190
Creating the Soft Toy Label	191
Requesting a Sample	192
Reflecting on the Process	193
Chapter Summary	193
26 Traditional Publishing	195
Submissions	197
Vanity Publishers	198
Self-publishing Stigma	199
Self-publishing Benefits	199
Chapter Summary	202
27 Glossary of Terms	203
28 Useful information	208
Epilogue	215

Preface

Welcome to my guide created to provide you with the essential knowledge to embark on your journey into the realm of writing children's literature and self-publishing.

How did it begin for me?

I've always dreamed of becoming an author, but life always seemed to have other plans. My stories remained tucked away in drafts, or in my imagination, waiting for the right moment to emerge. As my daughter grew older her enthusiasm for my storytelling continued to grow, sparking something inside me—a newfound inspiration that I couldn't ignore. This motivated me to finally turn my dream of becoming an author into a reality.

With my daughter's encouragement creating excitement I finally decided to take the plunge. I dusted off my ideas and began to breathe life into my long-held dream.

Starting on my journey as an author I initially found myself navigating unknown territory with little to no knowledge of the intricate world of book publishing. Despite this I eagerly embarked on the process of learning and discovery.

What I soon realised was that the path to achieving a published book was far more complex and broader than I had imagined. Armed with determination I started the process of uncovering various topics and gaining knowledge and experience. This took many months to build up the required knowledge, execute what I had learned, and finally publish my first book.

Now, I am eager to share the insights of my own journey to save you time and effort and to guide fellow aspiring authors on their path to success. This could potentially save you months and months off of your learning journey.

In the early stages of my journey I was undecided whether to try to pursue a traditional publishing contract or take the self-publishing route.

After reaching out to a select few publishers and receiving offers I carefully evaluated the terms. After careful consideration I made the decision to decline and opt for self-publishing. Maybe I will consider a publishing deal in the future however for now I am happy self-publishing.

As a result this book will be dedicated to exploring the self-publishing process.

Who am I?

My family originally came from Sunderland, Northeast England. My parents had the chance to emigrate to New Zealand, where they lived for several years. During that time they had their third daughter—me! When I was two we returned to the UK, where I have lived ever since. However, my family eventually decided to move back to New Zealand.

I now live in the East of England with my beautiful daughter, Bethany, and her dad, James, my Fiancé.

I am an avid reader and have always loved immersing myself in books from a young age. Growing up I would spend countless hours getting lost in different worlds, characters, and stories. The joy of discovering new adventures and gaining insights from various perspectives has been a constant source of inspiration. My love for reading has continued to fuel my imagination. I am pleased that my daughter also shares a love of books.

In my spare time I love to enjoy family activities. We often visit a variety of attractions, such as zoos, farm parks, or nature trails. Whether we're marvelling at exotic animals, interacting with farm animals, or simply enjoying a peaceful walk in the woods, these moments create cherished memories and often trigger lots of book ideas.

I have written and self-published multiple picture books that have entertained readers and achieved impressive sales figures. Many of my books have reached Amazon's best-selling status and have been ranked within the top ten in their respective book categories. I am also thrilled to say my books have also won book awards.

My stories have captivated audiences with their vibrant colours and uplifting stories, earning me a dedicated following of readers young and old.

With the experience I have gained I am very keen to share this to give you a solid foundation to commence your author journey. I would have loved to have discovered this information at the start of my own journey, as it would have saved me hours of time and probably helped me avoid a few mistakes along the way!

By the end of this guide I am confident that you will learn some great tips and information to start you on your journey.

You can follow my journey on social media:

- Facebook: https://www.facebook.com/rhymingmoments.co.uk
- Instagram: https://www.instagram.com/trudydavidsonauthor/
- tiktok: @trudydavidsonauthor
- linktree: https://linktr.ee/trudy.davidson
- My website: www.rhymingmoments.co.uk.

It is so exciting that you are reading this book, as it means you are keen and ready to start your writing journey! So grab a cuppa, turn the page and make a start.

All the best.

Trudy

1

Picture Book Definition and Key Areas

If you're starting from the beginning it's crucial to delve into what exactly constitutes a picture book. By now you've likely read a few, but if not, it's time to get started!

Engaging Stories with Illustrations

Let's begin with a high-level definition: A picture book is, as its title suggests, a combination of visual and written elements that tell a story. Primarily picture books are literature designed for children, with images playing a vital role in supporting the narrative.

Picture books cover a broad age range, typically from 2 years to approximately 8 years old. The complexity of the narrative and story further refines the book's target audience.

Picture books play a crucial role in a child's literacy progression. The interaction with the words and illustrations makes them a unique experience and one that many children should cherish. I bet there are many books you can still remember reading from your childhood. Ultimately your aim should be for the child to have a brilliant experience reading your book.

A Summary of Picture Book Essentials

Let's summarise the key areas of a picture book in a brief overview and then explore them in more detail throughout the guide:

Simplicity and Succinctness

Picture books usually use a simple and concise story-telling approach. Always keep in mind the word count for your target audience; choose your text carefully to convey the story within this word count limit. Later there will be a table with a guide to aim for the length of the story.

Age-appropriate Language

Part of the process of writing a picture book is to decide on your target audience. Once you have this set you need to use language appropriate for this age group and developmental stage. This includes the words you use along with how the sentences are structured.

Message, Morals, and Themes

Quite often picture books will be focused on a particular theme or message. For example, family, friendship, problem-solving, and moral lessons, to name a few. Consider themes that are of interest to children, and as you will read later, try to test your ideas by reading them to children, parents, friends, and teachers to see how they are perceived.

Read-Aloud Appeal

Picture books are ideal to read aloud especially as the target audience may not be reading yet themselves. They are interactive between the adult and child and the rhythmic flow of the story and the quality of the text need to contribute to a positive reading experience. So, reading your ideas aloud to potential readers and receivers of the story is an ideal way to test how the book flows. The reaction can be seen first-hand at each stage of the book.

Layout and Format

Pick up any picture book and you will immediately see that it has a distinctive format featuring both text and illustrations. The format and page layout are carefully designed to guide the reader through the narrative. The picture books that stand out often place the story carefully on each page to have a key stage of the story on every page turn. Clever use of design elements using varied font styles, page layouts, and highlighting keywords can bring additional focus to the story and give the reader an engaging and appealing experience as they read the book.

Emphasis on Strong Visuals

One of the key characteristics of picture books is the emphasis on the illustrations. The visuals are important to the story, provide context, add understanding to the text, and captivate the audience. When you get to the stage of deciding on the illustrations, and if you choose to hire an illustrator, take your time to find an illustrator that suits the look you had in mind. It might be that you try a few illustrators before deciding.

I began the visuals for my first book with a chosen illustrator. After completing several pages, I reflected and sought others' opinions. I decided it was not the style I wanted to continue with. I politely ended the agreement.

It is easy to get carried away when you see the book come to life, especially when it is your first; however, step back and reflect on the original illustration style you were setting out to achieve and gain other views too. Do this in the initial stages of working with an illustrator before continuing. Not getting this right from the start could be an expensive learning curve if you do decide to change your mind when the illustrations are part way through, or completed. We will cover more about illustrations later.

Appealing Characters

Illustrations will bring the characters to life making them visually appealing to young readers. Having relatable, fun, interesting, and memorable characters (to name a few options!) is a must.

2

Identify your audience

Deciding the Right Age Group for Your Picture Book

When creating a picture book one of the most crucial steps is identifying the right age group for your audience. This decision influences every aspect of your book, from the story and language, to the illustrations and overall design.

Understanding the developmental stages of children is fundamental in tailoring your content appropriately.

- For infants and toddlers books should feature simple, bright illustrations, and minimal text.
- Interactive elements like touch-and-feel, lift-the-flap, and sound buttons can enhance engagement.
- Preschoolers enjoy stories with simple plots, repetitive text, and rhyming words. The illustrations should be

colourful and detailed enough to spark their imagination without overwhelming them.
- As children move into the early school-age years they can handle more complex stories with deeper themes. The text can be longer and the illustrations can contain more details that they can explore.

Engaging your audience involves understanding what keeps children interested and entertained at each age.

- Interactive books are effective for infants and toddlers encouraging participation and learning through touch and exploration.
- Preschoolers enjoy repetitive phrases and predictable patterns that help them follow along and anticipate what comes next.
- Early school-age children are drawn to more complex narratives and enjoy elements of colourful, suspense, or mystery that challenge their thinking and keep them engaged.

Finding the right balance between education and entertainment is key to creating a successful picture book.

- For infants and toddlers focus on foundational learning, language development, and sensory experiences.
- Preschoolers benefit from educational content woven into fun stories that teach social skills and basic problem-solving.
- Early school-age children thrive on books that integrate advanced educational elements while providing an enter-

taining story that captures their imagination.

Identifying the right age group for your picture book is the first step in crafting a book that children will love and parents will appreciate.

How Long Should a Picture Book Be?

At this point I would like to touch on the length of the overall book, which also forms part of the appropriateness for the age range you have decided upon.

Picture books can vary in length, but usually, they are short stories.

A typical word count is somewhere in the range of 500–1,000 words, with many aiming to be around 700 words or less. Use the following information as a guide:

Standard Picture Book Length

Picture books are designed for children aged 2 to around 8 years old, featuring a word count typically between 500 and 1000 words. This range is carefully chosen to engage young readers without overwhelming them with too much text. The simplicity of language and the presence of colourful illustrations play a crucial role in captivating their attention and fostering early literacy skills. These books aim to entertain and educate, providing young children with enjoyable stories that encourage a love for reading from an early age.

Transitioning to Chapter Books

Children aged approximately 6 to 10 embark on a pivotal transition from picture books to more advanced chapter books, signifying a developmental shift in their reading abilities and interests. This stage introduces books with word counts typically ranging from 1,000 to 1,500 words, designed to engage young readers with slightly longer stories that begin to be more complex.

Tailoring Stories from Ages 2 to 8

- **Ages 2-4:** Simple stories with basic concepts, lots of repetition, and engaging illustrations.
- **Ages 4-6:** Slightly more complex narratives with a clear beginning, middle, and end, and relatable characters.
- **Ages 6-8:** More developed stories that may introduce simple plots and subplots, along with richer language and more detailed illustrations. This age range may also start to explore chapter books.

The Role and Significance of Illustrations in Picture Books

You need to bear in mind that picture books are visually telling stories. Therefore, illustrations play a significant role. The relationship between the text and illustrations is therefore so important. If you have too many words on a page this can deflect from the visuals. Try to use concise words and carefully select the text, ensuring the writing compliments the illustrations. The aim is for the child to have the best experience both visually and through the words on every page. However, remember that your audience will also include the adults reading the book, so it needs to be just as appealing to them as it is to the child.

Understanding Picture Book Buyers Through Statistics

I found it useful to research some statistics as to who is buying children's books. In the UK, the main buyers of children's books fall within the 30 to 44 age group. Females make up more than 70% of these buyers. Consider this when you start to look at the marketing for your book.

Nielsons also has interesting statistics.

The buyers behind the book sales – Nielsenbook-UK
   https://nielsonbook.co.uk/.

IDENTIFY YOUR AUDIENCE

Questions to Consider When Defining Your Audience

Think about the following questions:

- Who will buy your book?
- Why would they buy your book?
- Will your book be for girls or boys or both?
- What social media pages would the buyers follow?
- Where might they go to see your book advertised?
- Would your book content be useful as a classroom read?
- Will there be a lesson within your book of interest to the buyer?
- What topic will your book be based on and how many buyers would this appeal to?

The list could go on and on, but the key idea is to question whether your idea will sell and if there is a market out there that will buy it.

Talk to your target audience and potential buyers. Spend time with parents, teachers, and children to understand their preferences and needs.

Researching your audience is a significant factor in gathering valuable insights for your marketing plan later too.

Chapter Summary

- Decide on the target age range for your book.
- Keep in mind the word count guidelines.
- Tailor the language to your age range.
- Understand who would buy your book and why.
- Talk to your potential buyers.

3

Choose a message, a moral, or a theme

Exploring Themes, Messages and Morals in Picture Books

To start with, what is the difference between a message, a moral, and a theme?

Themes and messages are closely related but not exactly the same. Some of the concepts do intertwine, though.

What is a Theme?

A theme is a broader idea that runs throughout the story and is a central and recurring element. Depth to the story can be achieved, along with contributing to character development and plot progression. Themes could give differing perceptions or could give discussion points.

What is a Message?

A message can focus on a specific lesson, moral, or insight that the author would like to convey to the reader. It is usually more direct than a theme, and the text reflects this more prominently. A message is usually tied to a certain event or character's actions.

In summary

A theme is more like a broader topic, and a message would be more focused on a particular point.

What is a Moral?

A moral is a lesson or principle that teaches the difference between right and wrong or conveys a deeper understanding of ethical and virtuous behaviour. Morals often guide behaviour and decision-making by highlighting desirable conduct or values.

So, taking the high-level explanations consider whether you would like your picture book to convey a message, a moral, or a theme. You might, however, just have in mind a topic where the reader will learn something new, or just focus on writing a pure entertaining story!

Examples of Themes, Messages and Morals in My Picture Books

A few examples of the message, a moral, or a theme behind a couple of my picture books:

Rodney the Seagull - Chips, Ice-Cream and Cake - Rhyming Moments

```
Ultimately, I wanted a light-hearted picture book
aimed at the younger standard age range of picture
books.

The story revolves around a hilariously hungry
seagull who can't resist the delicious food people
are enjoying by the seaside. This cheeky bird swoops
down, trying to snatch meals right out of their
hands! We've all experienced those seaside moments
when a seagull gets a little too bold with our
snacks.

Unfortunately, Rodney is not very successful. After
landing on the pavement and squawking with
frustration, a passerby throws Rodney food.

Rodney starts trying to sing for his food, which is
more successful than stealing it.
```

Lucy Lamb's Most Curious Adventure – Rhyming Moments

```
So, the message within the book is about stealing,
but it is captured through the eyes of a hungry
seagull in a light-hearted way.
```

```
This delightful tale follows a curious lamb named
Lucy, who dreams of exploring beyond her field. When
a fallen tree creates a gap in the hedge, Lucy
seizes the chance to venture into the unknown with
her brother Harry by her side.

At first, Lucy feels nervous about the new
adventure. However, with Harry's encouraging words
she bravely pushes forward. As they roam the farm,
Lucy and Harry discover what all the animals do
throughout the day, learning fun animal facts along
the way.

This heartwarming story encourages children to
overcome their fears and try new things, which can
lead to making new friends. It's an entertaining
adventure packed with charming animal facts and
valuable lessons.
```

When I wrote this story I was already envisioning it as a series of adventures starring Lucy and her brother Harry. And why stop there? I imagined bringing these lovable characters to life as soft plush toys, perfect companions for young readers.

Both examples also came from personal experiences:

Rodney the Seagull - Chips, Ice-Cream and Cake - Rhyming Moments

```
The idea came from a family visit to the seaside,
where a very persistent seagull kept trying to steal
our food.

We each gave the seagull a name. My Daughter's
suggestion Rodney came out as the favourite.

The idea for the book grew from there and was based
on this actual seagull.

From this lighthearted moment the concept for the
book emerged, drawing inspiration from our amusing
encounter with Rodney the seagull.

It's funny how everyday experiences can inspire!
```

Lucy Lamb's Most Curious Adventure - Rhyming Moments

```
The concept came to life because my family and I
have always enjoyed visiting farm parks. Our
daughter is endlessly curious about the animals and
never hesitates to ask plenty of questions.

It was during one of these visits that the idea for
Lucy Lamb began to take shape, with Lucy herself
inspired by my daughter's inquisitive nature.
```

Drawing from Personal Experiences

I would therefore recommend drawing from your own personal experiences. Reflect on memories or be astute when you are out and about, as something may trigger an idea. Authenticity can add depth and make the story relatable to readers. It is also lovely to have a personal connection to your story.

Exploring Other Options and Considerations

- Identifying any interests or hobbies that you would like to focus on. Maybe with something to learn along the way. Children who are interested in these areas are more likely to want to engage with your book and to pick it up again and again.
- Consider whether you would like to cover any educational areas within your message, theme, or moral. For example, specific values, concepts, or life skills.
- Think about whether you would like to include any cultural considerations. Including a range of characters with various backgrounds, and family structures.
- Introducing some sort of problem or issue to overcome can add interest and give a great happy ending. You will find that many picture books will focus on some sort of obstacle.

Keeping up with the current trends in children's picture books and being aware of popular themes and writing styles may also lead you to decide which message, moral, or theme you would like to continue with.

Keep an eye out for illustration styles too. A simple web search for top-rated picture books brings up many books for you to browse through. Many of them will have a look-inside feature where you can read the first few pages, or take a trip to your local library.

Gaining feedback from parents, teachers, or children themselves about how your book idea might work is also a powerful addition to your planning. Ask for feedback on whether the story will resonate with children. Reading your manuscript to a child before proceeding further can be very insightful, as they will surely let you know what they think!

Keep in mind your target audience when you are thinking about a message, a moral, or a theme. The older picture book age range, for example, might require differing levels of complexity than the younger age range, who may prefer a more simple storyline.

The child may not be reading yet, and therefore the book will be read by an adult. Bear in mind that the story, although important to appeal to the child, must also interest the reader.

If anyone regularly reads to a child you know a child can have their favourite book that they want to read again and again. We have all been there and sometimes thought, 'Not this one again.' Then try to encourage the child to read another book, sometimes failing and other times resulting in choosing another book. You need to avoid this happening to your book! So, keep in mind that making the story equally appealing to adults plays a significant role too. The adults are also usually the ones who pick up the book in a shop to buy or search online for a book as a gift!

Chapter Summary

- Decide on a message, moral, or theme.
- Draw from personal experiences.
- Be astute to look around for triggers for ideas.
- Keep up-to-date with picture book trends.
- Gain feedback on your ideas.
- Always keep in mind your target audience.
- Make the story appealing to adults too.

4

The Ideas

Techniques to Spark Your Storytelling Journey

Whether you already have a clear idea for your story or need a bit of inspiration, here are some helpful techniques to get you started:

Lists to Generate Ideas for Your Picture Book

Begin with your overall message, moral, theme, or even just a word for your picture book idea. Jot down everything that comes to mind related to this message, moral, theme, or word. Start grouping these thoughts together to form associations and connections to spark ideas.

For example, if you start with the word "woodland," you might expand on it to create a theme involving a magical tale. Perhaps an elf embarks on a journey, interacting with various forest animals who offer to help. The forest itself, rich with unknown magic, presents challenges and adventures. Then start building on this overall idea.

SETTING	ATMOSPHERE	CHARACTERS	TYPE
Forest	Enchanting	Fairies	Journey
Trees	Whispering	Elves	Legend
Woodland	Moonlight	Deer	Quest
Moss	Ancient	Owls	Spell
Pathway	Magical	Squirrels	Tale
Thicket	Glimmering	Fox	
Clearing	Rustling	Hedgehog	
Cottage	Whimsical	Witch	
Brook	Shady	Wizard	
Stream		Rabbit	
Ferns		Oak Tree	
Maple		Birch Tree	
Oak		Maple Tree	
Mushrooms		Toadstools	

Mind Maps for Visualising Your Message, Moral, or Theme for Your Picture Book

If you've never used a mind map, it's a fantastic tool to try. If you're already familiar with it, consider using it to map out your message, moral, or theme. Place your idea in the middle then create branches to add related ideas and thoughts on characters, settings, and situations for your story. As you develop your mind map, start thinking about colours and images that can make your concept more visual and bring your idea to life. This can help you visualise the elements of your story and see how they connect.

A simple example using animals as a topic:

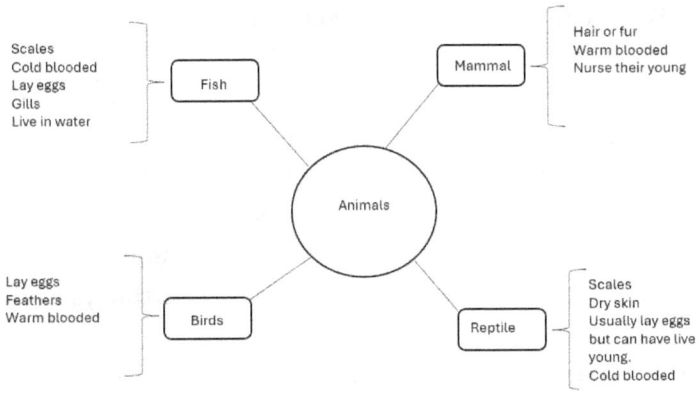

A mind map using animals as an example.

Here is a suggestion for a great tool for mind mapping. The app offers both a free version and a paid version, which has additional features. This can help you organise your thoughts, develop your ideas, and bring your story to life more effectively.

Check it out here:
   Xmind - Mind Mapping App

Drawing from Personal Experience

Think back to where you grew up:

- Was there anything quirky you remember?
- What was the surrounding area like?
- Anything you enjoyed doing?
- Were there places you liked to visit?
- Did you or your family or the people you lived with have anything that you remember that you could build on?
- Were there any unusual or amusing traditions? —maybe Uncle Sam liked to sing for each of your birthdays loudly and badly.
- Did you have any pets? Did they have any amusing habits?
- How about siblings?
- Any unusual hobbies?

This list could go on and on. As I write this, I find myself thinking about funny moments from my past. Enjoy taking some time out for this. It is amazing what will pop into your head.

Stories Inspired by My Own Experience

Some of my books were based on personal experiences, as mentioned earlier. For example:

My book "Lucy Lamb's Most Curious Adventure" was inspired by my family's frequent visits to farm parks and our young daughter's endless curiosity about the animals. My daughter loves exploring farms, and the main character, Lucy, is based on her.

Lucy Lamb's Most Curious Adventure - Rhyming Moments

Character Inspiration from Personal Experiences

Your inspiration doesn't have to come from places you've visited. Think about the people and events in your life that have left a lasting impression and consider how these experiences could form the basis of a relatable picture book.

A few suggestions that might help:

- You could try to begin to think of any interesting characters you may have met, maybe one you can recollect from your past.
- Think about their traits, personalities, and any quirks they may have.
- Imagine how these characters would interact with others and the world around them.
- Start to formulate the story around these characters and the relationships they may form.

Ask yourself.

- What if they did this?
- How would they react?
- How would others around them act?

Explore different questions to create various potential scenarios and consequences. This can trigger and help develop your storyline.

Observation for Inspiration

I find a wonderful way to pass the time is to discreetly watch people. Whether you're eating lunch on a bench or walking your dog, observe those around you and let your imagination run wild.

- Where are they going?
- What is their personality like?
- Do they have a family?
- Where might they live?

This can be a fantastic way to spark new ideas and create a compelling storyline.

Another option is to start with a setting first. Think about an interesting or unique place you may have visited. Then begin to imagine the world within this setting.

- What type of character might you see there?
- Why is this character in this setting?

Brainstorming with Others

If you have a rough idea of what you'd like to focus on, discuss it with friends or family. Gaining different perspectives and ideas can fuel your imagination and help expand your initial concept. Their insights might offer new angles or suggestions that you hadn't considered, enriching your story even further.

Creating Unforgettable Characters for Children

To create an unforgettable character for children, consider incorporating traits that are quirky, bold, or simply unique. Think about positive qualities like kindness, bravery, curiosity, or humour—traits children can admire and relate to.

Children often enjoy pretending to be characters from their favourite stories, so try to make your character relatable. Explore experiences such as going to school, making friends, or embarking on adventures that resonate with young readers.

Give your character opportunities to grow and learn throughout the story. Humour can also be a great way to entertain young readers and keep them amused.

Consider giving your character catchy phrases or perhaps a memorable song. Your book might become even more memorable and leave a lasting impression on children.

What Adults Look for in Children's Books

Adults are often the ones buying children's books. Consider what parents, teachers, and caregivers might value in the books they choose for children.

Consider themes or topics that align with important life lessons or values parents want to instil in their children.

Books that include kindness, resilience, diversity, or environmental awareness might prompt adults to discuss them with others.

Ultimately, creating a book that resonates with children and adults can lead to word-of-mouth recommendations and positive reviews, encouraging others to explore your book and ultimately buy it.

Relax and Spark Creativity

Sometimes, the best way to spark creativity is to take a moment to relax, sit back, and let your imagination run wild. Make yourself a nice cup of tea and let your thoughts flow freely. Keep a pen and paper, your phone for notes, or a recorder handy to capture any ideas that come to mind. As your thoughts begin to flow it's crucial to be ready to capture them, especially if you start to develop ideas for text. Whether it's jotting down notes or recording voice memos, having a way to preserve your ideas ensures that you don't lose any of those creative sparks.

This is a little rhyme I pulled together when I was at the start of my journey about this very topic:

> *Ideas for a book can be everywhere.*
> *Sit back and relax in a chair.*
> *Look around... What do you see?*
> *A colourful orange and black bee.*
> *Let's write a story about this little fellow.*
> *Maybe he could be learning the cello!*
> *A dog goes by; does he wink as he passes?*
> *A story about his secret agent classes!*
> *A cloud passes up above, quickly changing shape.*
> *Maybe there's a trapped bird inside trying to escape?*
> *It flew in the cloud, chasing a balloon.*
> *Which floated up after it was let go by a raccoon?!*
> *You spot a caterpillar on a branch.*
> *Maybe it grew up on a ranch?*
> *And wanted a change, so caught a bus?*
> *But now they wish they were home. Oh, what a fuss!*
> *So, while you are sitting on the bench, just enjoy.*
> *Maybe imagine you're on a boat... Ship ahoy!*
> *Just let your imagination run free.*
> *And jot down a few ideas—maybe three!*

Books are a wonderful way to escape.
and a lot of fun to think about and shape.
There is a book idea for everyone.
Enjoy the author's imagination and have fun!

Chapter Summary

```
- Try different techniques to trigger your idea or
to expand on it.
- Draw from your own experiences and memories.
- Gain feedback on your idea.
- Take time out to relax and let your thoughts run
free.
- Make sure you have a tool to record your ideas.
```

5

Create a compelling story

Developing a Simple and Engaging Plot

Now comes the part about creating the story. Devising a simple, engaging plot can be a critical factor in the success of a picture book. The message, theme, or moral you have decided on will be the focus of your story and will guide the development of the narrative, along with the actions your characters will take. Deciding on your characters and making them memorable so they connect with your target audience is essential. Establish their role throughout your book and keep it consistent. It is worth investing the time to ensure the characters are right from the beginning. Since you are writing a picture book, this shouldn't take too long to draft out or conceptualise.

Creating Characters for Book Series Potential

Useful tip: Create a character or two that can be reused for potential follow-on books, allowing you to create a series if you wish to.

I had this vision for my book, "Lucy Lamb's Most Curious Adventure".

Lucy Lamb's Most Curious Adventure - Rhyming Moments

I always had the aim of creating a series, as well as plush toys out of the characters. Also, think about merchandise opportunities for your characters. There is a chapter dedicated to my plush toy journey.

A high majority of picture books focus on a plot that involves a challenge or some kind of conflict. The characters must work through this, and this drives the story forward.

Examples of Themes in My Picture Books

An example from my book, "Mr. Vole's Upside-Down New Pots".

Mr Vole's Upside-Down New Pots - Rhyming Moments

The Theme: I set out to create a picture book that would teach children a memory technique through rhyme. The rhyme used in the book is one I learned at school, and I must admit, I have used rhyme to remember many things since! I also wanted to incorporate themes of friendship and helping each other, featuring characters who are unlikely to be friends. Additionally, I aimed to include an element of learning with some fun animal facts along the way.

The Setting: I chose a woodland setting.

The Characters: I selected an owl, a vole, and a sly fox for the main characters.

The Plot: The owl is wise, and animals visit his tree for advice. The answers are animal facts. However, the owl has one weakness, he cannot remember anything about the planets in the sky.

The vole, who makes pots, sees all the visitors and decides to move into the roots of Ollie the Owl's tree to try to sell his pots to them. The vole keeps the pots upside down so he can hide under them from the owl.

One day, while peeping through a hole in one of the pots, the vole asks the owl if he knows the answer to any question. The owl admits he cannot remember what is in the sky. A sly fox hears this and decides to use this information to his advantage to try to make the owl lose his status as the wisest owl.

In the end, the vole helps the owl with a clever rhyme to remember the order of the planets, and the fox does not prevail.

The rhyme that forms part of the book title "Mr. Vole Earns Money Just Selling Upside Down New Pots" uses the first letters to represent the order of the planets. (P for Pots can no longer be included due to Pluto no longer being classed as a planet, a great talking point at school visits).

The various events within your book can build interest for your reader. Think about how each event will contribute to wanting the reader to know what happens in the end. Children love to guess what might happen next.

There is usually a turning point within the book, which is the crucial moment in the story where the characters face a decision or have a revelation. The turning point or revelation often sets the scene for the resolution, and the plot takes a turn.

Embracing Happy Endings in Picture Books

Ensure you complete the book with a satisfying resolution. Always keep in mind that picture books usually have a happy ending!

Taking the example of "Mr. Vole's upside-down New Pots".

Mr Vole's Upside-Down New Pots - Rhyming Moments

- **Building interest:** Early in the book the fox hears the conversation between the owl and the vole. Throughout the book you wonder when the fox will make his appearance.

Children have said they have enjoyed spotting the fox on the pages.
- **Turning point:** The fox joins the queue of animals, waiting his turn to ask the question that he thinks will catch the owl out. However, he does not know the vole is near and is able to give the owl a big hint to help him answer the question correctly.
- **Resolution**: The fox does not succeed in making the owl look less clever in front of the queue of animals. The vole helps, and in doing so, he becomes friends with the owl who lets him continue living in the roots of his tree to sell his pots. They become good friends.

Aligning Plot Complexity with Your Target Age Group in Picture Books

Ensure that the complexity of the plot aligns with the age group you are targeting. Picture books for younger children will naturally have simpler plots than those intended for older children. Although "Mr. Vole's Upside-Down New Pots" targeted the standard picture book age, I targeted the higher age range for this book due to the complexity of the plot. This book has been a hit when I have read it at school visits as I include a focus on the order of the planets and why Pluto is no longer a planet.

Reading Your Draft to Your Target Audience

Consider reading your draft to your target audience. To name a few: children, teachers, and parents to gain feedback. Sharing in this way will always give you a good idea of whether the plot is one that will be successful with your target audience once published.

Your book is your own personal creativity and is unique to you. Grab the ideas you have and have fun creating them.

Chapter Summary

- Devise a simple, engaging story.
- Choose a suitable story for your target age range.
- Your chosen theme, message, or moral will guide the plot.
- Aim for memorable characters.
- Consider potential merchandise.
- Keep in mind whether you would like to aim for a series.
- Build interest throughout the book.
- Consider sharing or reading your drafts for feedback.
- Conclude on a happy note.

6

Layout And Format

There is no set answer for which layout and format you should use, as formats can vary. I can provide the format I've chosen, which seems to be the typical picture book layout. Consider printing costs at this stage, especially for self-publishing, as the size and length of your book can impact the printing cost.

Choosing the Right Layout and Format for Your Picture Book

Picture books tend to be 32 pages long. This includes:

Title pages

- The title pages include the book's title, author's name, and illustrator's name. It is one of the first pages readers see when they open the book.

Copyright page.

- This page provides information about the book's publication, copyright, and ISBN details. It could include other things like disclaimers and other legal information.

Endpapers.

- These are the pages on the other side of the cover. Usually, these are blank; however, some picture books have added pictures or patterns.

Creating Meaningful Dedications in Your Picture Book

Picture books tend to be dedicated to someone or something special. A dedication can be from the author only or from the illustrator too. I decided to put my dedications at the top of my copyright page.

A couple of examples to who I made dedications:

- For Bethany. Thank you for making each day a happy adventure.
- For the children who will lead the way for a cleaner and greener world, small gestures together make a big difference.

A Pictorial Guide to a 32-Page Picture Book

Let's explore the pictorial form of a picture book layout. I created this using PowerPoint when I started, finding it useful to have a visual reference. It depicts a standard 32-page picture book.

32 Page Picture Book Layout

	Front cover	Inside front cover	Title + spot image	Copyright	Main Title page	Story	Story
Story	Story	Story	Story	Story	Story	Story	Story
Story	Story	Story	Story	Story	Story	Story	Story
Story	Story	Story	Story	Story	Story	End papers	Inside front cover	Back cover

Key Picture Book Sections Explained

Let us have a look at each section in more detail.

Front cover: The front cover is the first thing potential readers and buyers see. It is the initial impression of the book and plays a significant role in attracting attention. Ensure you have a well-designed cover to encourage readers to pick up your book.

You can:

- design this yourself.
- hire someone to design it for you.
- or leave it to your illustrator, with guidance from you.

I thoroughly enjoy taking time to think about the cover design. I find creating the cover design and sketching a few ideas with pencil and paper enjoyable. Once it looks like what I had in mind and is a good enough sketch, I pass it on to the illustrator. Alternatively, I sometimes write a description for the illustrator to follow. However, you will discover the recommendation is to seek a professional to design this for you, as it is crucial to get it right. I still like to be involved and collaborate with the illustrator. I took this risk, and official reviews from book award panels highlighted that the book covers look professionally designed. Based on this feedback I will continue designing the book covers for now.

Endpaper/simple title page: The other side of the front cover is usually blank; however, some authors decide to add a pattern. I decided to go with the majority and leave this blank.

Then comes the simple title page. The simple title page usually consists of the title and a simple illustration.

Copyright text/main title page: The copyright text is usually on the left side.

After lots of research online as to what to include within the copyright text, I decided to develop the text myself. You will also find lots of examples in the many picture books that have been published. Most are pretty much the same. There is also the option of consulting with legal professionals.

The copyright text is a crucial part of any book as it protects the author's and illustrator's rights. The copyright text may vary as some aspects of the text are specific to your book.

Let's take a look at the common elements:

- The symbol © or the words Copyright.
- Year of publication.
- Name of who the copyright is referring to (usually the author and illustrator).
- ISBN, the International Standard Book Number, More about this later.
- Stating that a CIP catalogue of the book is available from the British Library. CIP stands for Cataloguing in Publication. CIP is a bibliographic record prepared by the Library of Congress and allocated to a book before it is published. In the United Kingdom, you are required to send a copy of each publication to the British Library under legal deposit regulations. Legal deposit is a legal requirement for publishers to submit copies of their publications to designated national libraries or institutions.
- The purpose of legal deposit is to ensure that a comprehensive collection of the nation's published output is preserved for future generations. This topic will be covered again later in the book.

- Edition number, if applicable.
- Recognising the illustrator or anyone else who may have contributed to the book. As mentioned earlier, I decided to also have my book dedication at the top of the copyright text page.
- Any disclaimers. The most common one is "All rights reserved. No part of this book may be reproduced or transmitted in any form by any means, electronic or mechanical, including photocopying, recording, or any information storage and retrieval system, without permission in writing from the author (or publisher)".

This is the outcome of my research, but always validate the information to ensure that it is the most current and suitable for your book.

The main title page is usually to the right of the copyright text and has the book's title again. Usually, a simple illustration will accompany the title, along with the author's and illustrator's names. It may also state the publisher's details, if applicable. I mention Rhyming Moments, which is my publishing company.

The main story: The next 12-page double spread is the actual story.

Simple spot image/endpapers: A simple spot image is a small, stand-alone illustration. Endpapers are the pages on the inside covers of a printed book, both at the front and the back. Children's picture books often feature illustrations or patterns that relate to the book's theme or story, but this is not required and can add additional cost when printing.

Back cover: Just like the front cover, the back cover is important for catching the attention of potential buyers. It usually includes:

- A summary of the book's plot, theme, or key elements.
- Barcode and ISBN (International Standard Book Number) for retailers and cataloguing purposes.
- Option to have the author's bio and picture, personal choice. Some books also have this on the inside front or back cover.
- If you can obtain reviews, testimonials, and endorsements from notable figures and critics, these can be referenced too.
- It is optional to add other books you have written, but this is a great marketing opportunity for potential further sales.
- Publisher details, as applicable. As mentioned, I have added my publishing company "Rhyming Moments".
- It is optional to have a QR code that links to your website.
- I have also seen authors use calls to action. A call to action (CTA) is a prompt that encourages a response or action. This could be placed anywhere on the back cover or at the end of the book. A common example is asking the reader to leave a review if they enjoyed the book.

This is a standard 32-page picture book to use as a basis. Sometimes this will not work for your book, so adapt it to suit.

For example, some of my books have 14-page double spreads for the story. When I started to map out which text would be positioned on which page, 12-pages did not work, so I needed to add a further two pages to not spoil the book's flow and to limit the text per page.

Complete some research and look at other children's picture books to get an idea of the number of pages, general word count, and amount of illustrations used. This information will give you a guide for your book.

A little tip: Consider whether you would like to display the price on the back of your book.

A few things to consider:

- If print costs rise you may need to alter your book price. This would mean an adjustment to your cover each time, as the price stated would be incorrect.
- If you are to distribute your book worldwide it also avoids having the incorrect currency stated.
- Be aware that the main online selling platforms can increase or decrease the cost of your book. You will keep the same amount of compensation; however, any additional profit or loss will be at the online selling platform's end. This can be to your advantage if they decide to decrease the cost, as it is a good opportunity to market your book as being at a temporary discounted rate. However, it is more of a challenge if the price is increased for a limited time as this may put off potential buyers. Your stated book price will therefore be inaccurate.

Once you have more than one book published, consider adding information about your other books to the inside front or back cover. If readers, both adults and children, enjoy your book they often become interested in your other work. This is a perfect opportunity to market your other titles and include your website if you have one. You could also offer an incentive, such as free colouring pages or activity sheets, to encourage visits to your website.

At the end of this book there are some suggested tools that you may like to explore and ones I find useful.

Chapter Summary

```
- There is no set format and layout for a picture
book.
- Use a 32-page picture book layout as a guide, but
ultimately the page count will be dictated by the
length of your book.
- Think about what you would like to display before
and after the story.
- The cover is critical, as this is the first
impression buyers have of your book.
- Look at other picture book formats and layouts to
give you ideas.
```

7

Copyright

Copyright Information

For the most up-to-date information on copyright I recommend visiting the government's official website. Their pages on copyright provide comprehensive and current details on the subject, including guidelines, laws, and procedures related to copyright protection. This resource is invaluable for understanding your rights and responsibilities, as well as for ensuring that you are compliant with the latest regulations.

Intellectual property: Copyright - GOV.UK (www.gov.uk)

Disclaimer: Please note I am not a legal expert or qualified in this area in anyway. I did research copyright laws when embarking on my publishing journey. I recommend you do the same to ensure you have the most up-to-date and accurate information.

Copyright is a legal concept that provides the creator of the original work with exclusive rights to use and distribute it, and typically, this lasts a lifetime of at least 70 years. It should grant the creator control over how their work is reproduced, distributed, performed, and displayed, preventing others from using it without permission.

When I started, I signed up with a company where I could upload files to document how my ideas developed and provide evidence of when I created them. If anyone made claims about my work I could present this evidence. This service was optional and came at a minimal expense. As my experience grew I found it unnecessary. Copyright protection is granted automatically upon the creation of an original work, and no formal registration is required, although it remains an option.

It goes without saying to include a copyright notice or symbol in all your books, the year of publication, and the copyright owner's name (for example, you as the author and the illustrator's name). State clearly how others can use your work and when permission is required.

As mentioned earlier, you can write your copyrighted text or hire someone to assist you.

A Useful Article on Copyright

https://www.societyofauthors.org/advice/guides/

Use the Copyright Symbol

When you distribute your work to others for any reason, make sure to display the copyright symbol (©). This helps to assert your rights and indicate that the work is protected. If you are unsure about how to use the copyright symbol or need more information on copyright issues, it is advisable to seek professional advice.

Placement of Copyright Information in Your Book

Typically, the copyright text is found at the front of the book before the story begins. This text usually includes the copyright symbol, the year of publication, and the name of the copyright holder. Additionally, it may contain statements regarding rights reserved, permissions, and any relevant disclaimers. Ensuring this information is clearly displayed helps protect your work and informs readers of your legal rights. Here is an example of the wording I use:

COPYRIGHT

For Bethany
Thankyou for making each day a happy adventure.

rhymingmoments.co.uk
First published 2021 by Rhyming Moment's books
61 Bridge Street, Kington HR5 3DJ

ISBN: 978-1-9196188-2-1

Text copyright © Trudy Davidson 2021
Illustrations copyright © Melanie Mitchell 2021
The rights of Trudy Davidson and Melanie Mitchell to be
identified as the author and illustrator of this work
have been asserted in accordance with the
Copyright, Designs and Patents Act 1988.

All rights reserved. No part of this publication may be
reproduced, stored in a retrieval system or transmitted
in any form, or by any means (electronic, mechanical,
photocopying, recording or otherwise), without the prior
written permission of the publisher.

A CIP catalogue for this book is
available from the British Library
upon request.

Chapter Summary

- Use the appropriate copyright symbols and text within your publication and when issuing it to others.
- If you are unsure or need guidance on copyright, seek advice from a legal professional.

8

Book Size (Trim Size)

Choosing the Right Trim Size for Your Picture Book

You will find various book sizes, referred to as trim sizes, for picture books. Here are some key areas to consider when deciding the size of your book.

- Remember, picture books are for younger children, and having larger dimensions may be better for visibility.
- A larger text size can be more suitable for younger readers. Ensuring the text remains easily readable and covering age-appropriate readability needs.
- The length of your book can impact its overall size. A shorter picture book story typically results in fewer pages, whereas longer narratives may naturally require more. However, the number of pages can also be influenced by the amount of text per page and size of illustrations.
- Illustrations are a critical factor. If your illustrations are

intricate, a larger picture book format may better showcase their details, making them visually captivating for readers. However, many excellent picture books with large illustrations and text look brilliant. I highly recommend exploring a wide range of picture books—not to copy, but to inspire your decision on how to size your book according to your concept.
- You could try to have a go at creating mock-ups in varied sizes to see which fits your book the best. For your first book, it might be a worthwhile investment of time.
- If you plan to release a series, consider the book size to be consistent with future releases.

The Importance of Book Size

The book size is especially important, as it affects your printing costs.

If you choose the self-published route, I am sure you will aim to upload your manuscript to online selling platforms. These give you the option to print your picture book on demand. You do have the option of distributing your book yourself. However, consider costs for holding stock and postage, space for stock, and your time. For my picture books, I selected print-on-demand. I also keep my stock for website sales and for selling at events.

Print-on-demand (POD) allows for a book to be printed and fulfilled only when an order is placed by a customer. This method eliminates the need for distributors to maintain stock of your book. Consequently, there are no upfront costs associated with stocking inventory, and your book can be available for sale immediately upon upload. By printing books on demand, it minimises excess ordering, storage, distribution costs, and potential waste in case of revisions to the book.

Be aware that print-on-demand costs are typically calculated based on the page count of your book, influenced by the chosen trim size (book size). Factors such as the print quality selected can also impact the overall cost.

After looking at various sizes of picture books and considering the length of my books with illustrations, I decided upon 8.5 x 11 inches for all my picture books so far.

To give you an example of print costs for this size through one of the major selling platforms. The hard-cover print cost is £7.00 upwards, and the softcover print cost is £2.40 upwards. The print cost and the amount the platforms retain will steer the book price, as you would also like a profit from the book sale!

Various online calculators will give you an idea of the revenue generated, I would recommend using these to gain up-to-date costs, as these can change.

Some authors, however, do go down the route of distributing themselves. I would recommend looking into both options to see if there would be any cost savings, which would include looking into companies that can supply you with printed copies of your book. Most printers will have a minimum order amount, so you will also need to consider where to store the books. Postage is also a factor to consider, as this may limit where you distribute. The benefit of having a print-on-demand service is that it will be distributed worldwide and use printers within the locations of the buyer to print and distribute the books. Just to add, I do hold stock of my books to fulfil website orders and to also take them along to any book fairs. I also hold stock for school visits and other author visits for the potential sales they generate.

I would recommend that if you are going to self-publish, familiarise yourself with print costs and make sure you do not choose a non-standard trim size that could potentially cost more to print.

Print Cost Online Calculator

The main online selling platforms all have calculators for you to enter the book size to inform you of the compensation you will receive. They will also have a list of the standard book sizes (trim sizes).

myaccount.ingramspark.com/Portal/Tools/PubCompCalculator

At this point, it is also worth mentioning that the gutter is the centre of the book where the pages are bound. It is important to ensure that your illustrations take this into account and that no essential parts of the picture are lost when printed.

Chapter Summary

```
- There is no set answer for what the size of your
book should be.
- The optimal size will depend on the unique aspects
of your book.
- Take the time to explore assorted sizes and
associated costs.
- Compare the costs of using print on demand and
distributing yourself, or, like me, a mixture of
both.
- Utilise the online calculator for compensation.
```

9

The Rough Draft

Choosing Your Writing Style

Once you have the idea chosen, the next step is creating your first draft. Consider which writing style you would like to apply.

Types of Rhyme in Writing

If you are considering using rhyme, there are various types to choose from:

End Rhyme

Rhymes that occur at the ends of lines.
Example:
She set off on her journey, which she made every **day**, practising her singing and ballet along the **way**.

Internal Rhyme

Rhymes that occur within a single line or between internal phrases across multiple lines.
Example:
Once upon a midnight **dreary**, while I pondered, weak and **weary**

Perfect Rhyme (or Exact Rhyme)

Rhymes where the sounds are exactly the same.
Example:
Jump and Hump.

Slant Rhyme (or Near Rhyme)

Rhymes where the sounds are similar but not exactly the same.
Example: Bridge and grudge, Shape and keep.

These pairs demonstrate slant rhyme because they share some degree of similarity in sound. "bridge" and "grudge" share the ending "-idge" and "-udge" sounds, while "shape" and "keep" have similar ending sounds "-ape" and "-eep".

Eye Rhyme

Rhymes that look like they should rhyme based on spelling but do not rhyme when pronounced.
   Example: Love and move, Cough and bough.

Rich Rhyme

Rhymes where the words are homophones (they sound the same but have different meanings).
   Example: Break and brake, Pair and pear.

Identical Rhyme

Rhymes that use the same word twice.
   Example: "two" and "too," or "ball" and "bawl."

Masculine Rhyme

Rhymes that end on a stressed syllable.
   Example: The dog barked loud in a crowd.

Feminine Rhyme

Rhymes that end on an unstressed syllable, often involving two or more syllables.
Example:
Yankee Doodle went to town
A-riding on a **pony**
He stuck a feather in his hat
And called it **macaroni**

As you read the song, you will find the last rhyming words are feminine rhymes. They have the unstressed syllables in the ending such as in "pony" and "macaroni".

Monorhyme

Monorhyme refers to the use of the same end-sound within multiple lines of a poem. Usually, the term describes poems that only use one end sound.
Example:
The night was cold and **bold.**
Stories of old were **told,**
and Treasures of gold **unfold.**

Chain Rhyme

Rhymes where the ending syllable of one line rhymes with the beginning syllable of the next.
Example:
*Nerve thy soul with doctrines **noble**,*
***Noble** in the walks of time,*

If you are thinking about writing a rhyming story, consider which rhyme scheme or pattern you'd like to use.

Past and Present Tense

Both present and past tenses have unique advantages that can make a story appealing to children. Lets take a look at each one:

Present Tense

The present tense makes the story feel like it's happening right now, creating a sense of immediacy and excitement. This can be particularly engaging for young readers who might feel more involved in the action. By narrating events as they unfold, the present tense can make children feel like they are part of the story experiencing events alongside the characters.

Present tense often leads to more vivid and detailed descriptions helping children visualise the scenes better. The sense of ongoing action can make the narrative more dynamic and captivating, drawing the reader into the story world. This vivid imagery allows children to see, hear, and feel what the characters are experiencing, making the story more immersive.

The present tense can heighten emotional responses making the reader feel more of what the characters are feeling. For example, "Sophie runs through the forest, her heart pounding with excitement. She can hear the birds singing and the leaves rustling in the breeze." This approach can make the reading experience more engaging for young readers.

A great article from my research:
Writing in Present Tense: The Secret to This Popular Writing Style (kindlepreneur.com)

Past Tense

When we tell each other stories we naturally speak in the past tense. If you wanted to tell someone what happened to you at work or yesterday driving to the shops, you wouldn't tell them about it as if it was happening right now. Because it happened in the past, you would tell them about it using the past tense.

This natural tendency is perhaps the best explanation for why writing fiction in the past tense is so common.

Many classic children's books are written in past tense. The past tense aligns with the traditional narrative style of "once upon a time" stories. It allows for a clear beginning, middle, and end, helping children understand the structure of a story.

A great article from my research:
   Past Tense Writing: The Secret to This Popular Writing Style (kindlepreneur.com)

Conclusion for past and present tense

In children's picture books, the choice between using past or present tense depends on how you want to tell the story to young readers. Whether you use past tense to recount events that have already happened, or present tense to make the story feel like it's unfolding right now, each option brings its own unique way to engage and delight young imaginations. You will find the majority of picture books use past tense.

A great article from my research:
   You searched for present tense | Kindlepreneur

First Person or Third Person

When writing a children's book choosing between first person and third person narrative can significantly impact how young readers connect with the story. Lets take a look at each one:

First Person

A first-person narrative in a picture book means telling the story from the perspective of the main character using "I" or "we." This allows young readers to see and experience the events directly through the eyes of the character. It creates a personal connection between the reader and the story, making the adventure, challenges, and victories feel more immediate and relatable.

In a first-person narrative, the main character becomes the storyteller, sharing their thoughts, feelings, and experiences as they unfold. This perspective can engage young readers by inviting them into the character's world, fostering empathy as they understand the character's emotions and motivations first-hand.

Third person

A third-person in a picture book means telling the story by a narrator who is not a character in the story. This narrator uses pronouns like "he," "she," or "they" to refer to the characters. Unlike first-person, where the main character tells the story directly, third-person provides a broader perspective by describing the actions, thoughts, and feelings of characters from an outside viewpoint.

With third-person narration, young readers observe the story unfolding as if watching it from the outside.

Using third-person in a picture book can offer flexibility in storytelling, as it allows authors to explore multiple characters' perspectives and settings without being limited to one character's viewpoint. It can create a sense of curiosity and anticipation as readers follow different characters' journeys and discover how their actions contribute to the story's outcome.

For young children, third-person narrative can provide a balanced and engaging storytelling experience, allowing them to explore various characters and settings while maintaining a clear narrative structure.

Conclusion for first or third person

First Person is ideal for creating an intimate, personal connection with the main character and offering a unique, engaging voice. It's particularly effective if the story revolves around the inner thoughts and feelings of the main character.

Third Person provides greater narrative flexibility, allowing for multiple viewpoints and a broader perspective. It's well-suited for traditional storytelling. My picture books are all third person.

There is no correct answer for which style you choose consider your story's needs, your target audience, and the type of connection you want to establish. You may simply prefer to write in a specific style. The majority of picture books I have read are third person.

Crafting Your Picture Book with Style and Audience in Mind

Begin to write with your chosen style in mind, along with the age group you are writing for. Try to keep track of your word count as you go. Alternatively, review at the end to see if you need to trim the word count. I personally prefer to keep track as I go.

At this stage just start writing. It doesn't need to be perfect. Begin by creating the story. Once you get started you will find that your ideas for the book will naturally come together and flow as you work through each stage of the writing process. Start to refine the theme, morale or message you have chosen and begin to outline your story.

You may have started to do this already in your pre-work; however, at the writing stage, your character's personalities will start to take shape, deciding what features they may have and whether they have any traits. The visualisation of the characters will form in your mind as the writing progresses. Make a note as you go of these features and characteristics, as you may want to pass them on to the illustrator.

Once you have the manuscript in its first draft, take your time to go back through it and refine it multiple times. I found it advantageous to revise and edit, then leave it for a couple of days, and then go through the process again.

Picture books are often read aloud to children. Reading aloud to ensure the text flows is therefore essential to ensure the text works well in this format.

Gathering Feedback

Asking others to read your book for their views too is useful. Just be mindful that everyone has an opinion and different ideas. Listen and consider the feedback; however, ensure you are choosing to incorporate the views that keep the draft in line with your idea and the flow of the book you set out to do.

Dedicating time to this process proves invaluable, so I consistently prioritise it. I have a personal example to share with you. When I asked a relative to review "Elephant May's Most Slippery Day" they highlighted a crucial detail I intended to revise. In my initial draft I assigned temporary names to the animals to shape the story. I planned to go back to change them starting with the corresponding letter ('B' for buffalo, 'L' for lion, etc.). However, as I became accustomed to these placeholder names I nearly overlooked this step. My very helpful relative, unaware of my plan, suggested aligning the names accordingly, which served as a reminder. This also highlights the importance of making notes during drafting to ensure no details are overlooked.

Reading your draft to your target audience is also an ideal way to gain feedback from your readers. I enjoyed reading the draft to my daughter and her friends to see if they liked the story and ask if they would change anything. It is brilliant what children can suggest and notice. Just consider that picture books are visual and reading text alone to children can sometimes get a different reaction. As you read the draft be aware of how engaged the children are, whether there were any words that they didn't understand, and what sort of questions they asked. All of this may make you tweak certain parts of the book or validate that the story gains the reaction you desired.

Overcoming Writer's Block

At some point you might stare at your screen or paper, and nothing comes to mind, or you might write one sentence or two in a day! Do not worry; I am sure it happens to most of us. Go for a walk, take a break, and return to it later. You will find that the creative juices will start flowing again, and it is a temporary pause.

It is a lovely feeling to see your ideas start to come together as a story. One day you will pick up your published book and think, "I did that".

Chapter Summary

- Decide on your writing style.
- Track your word count.
- Just start writing, and you will find it will start to flow.
- Capture ideas to share with your illustrator.
- Keep in mind your target age group.
- Read your draft to others.
- Take breaks when needed.
- Enjoy the creativity of writing!

10

Self-Editing

Editing Your Draft to Refine Your Final Version

This part of the process is a vital stage. It is reading and re-reading your draft repeatedly to polish it to be your final version before issuing the document to a professional editor and proofreader. Hiring a professional after you have reviewed your book is your choice, however I would highly recommend it.

I find it useful to step away for a while before starting the editing, giving yourself a chance to come back with fresh eyes. Utilise spellcheck and grammar tools; however, I would propose not to rely on these, so start with this to capture the obvious and then complete your editing stages.

As mentioned previously, read your draft aloud. This can help you spot errors or possible awkward phrasing and inconsistencies. I find reading aloud engages you differently than reading silently and helps you notice things you might have missed. I also find you focus more on the words when you read them aloud.

Split the editing process down. One read-through focused on the plot. The next read will focus on structure; the next read will focus on characters; the next will focus on grammar; and so on. For a picture book this will not take long.

When you focus on the characters, you need to check for consistency. Ensure that key aspects remain throughout. For example, if you have described your character as being tall at the start unless there is a reason they may have lost height, then they should remain tall throughout! When the illustrations commence ensure the same hair colour, eye colour, and features continue to be used unless the story warrants them changing.

After each read I would rest before starting the next read. I find this keeps your objective perspective on track.

Try to review, and trim any unnecessary words, sentences, or paragraphs. This is particularly important if you need to slim the word count down.

Enhancing Your Manuscript with Outside Perspectives

A recurring theme throughout this book is obtaining feedback, and it is mentioned again here. Let friends, family, teachers, and fellow authors, to name a few, read your manuscript to provide feedback on anything they would alter. When you write, it is amazing what you write and what others spot that you do not.

For example, in my "Lucy Lamb's Most Curious Adventure" rough draft, I had put baa'd, as in the moment of writing it seemed a valid word to describe the voice of a sheep. My mum quite rightly pointed out that it should be bleated, as baa'd is not a word! I find it amusing and brilliant how you can get so caught up when writing and add these oversights. Always be open to feedback. This is my favourite example and I am happy to share it as it still amuses me.

Keep repeating this process until you are happy with your final draft.

Chapter Summary

- Self-editing is an iterative process.
- It is beneficial to have multiple rounds of editing focusing on various aspects.
- Take a rest in between reads.
- Reading your story aloud will be beneficial.
- Gain feedback.

11

Professional Editing

Hiring a Professional Editor

Now that you are happy with your final draft the next step is hiring a professional editor, which is a valuable part of the process. You might be unsure whether to hire an editor, especially after thoroughly checking your work. However, this is a worthwhile investment to ensure that your book is the best it can be, helping you refine and enhance your manuscript. No author wants to receive bad feedback due to spelling and other errors that may remain within your book.

So far, I have hired editors who charge per word rather than an hourly rate. However, some have a minimum word count requirement. For picture books, which often have lower word counts, you might need to pay for the minimum word count even if your manuscript is shorter.

There are different types of editing. Here is a brief overview of each one:

Development Editing

Development editing focuses on the overall structure and content. The outcome of the development editing stage is to help the author shape and refine their book into a cohesive, compelling story.

A developmental editor will look at the elements of the book, such as plot, pacing, character development, and theme, and provide feedback and suggestions for improvement. The editor may make suggestions for cutting or adding material and restructuring the book to make it more effective and engaging.

This type of editing is particularly important for authors who have a rough draft of their book and are looking to improve its overall quality and readability. It's also a great way to get an outside perspective on your book and identify areas for improvement that you may not have considered.

Line Editing

Line editing is a type of editing that focuses on the individual lines of text in a manuscript. The goal of line editing is to improve the flow and readability of the text by making changes to sentence structure, word choice, and phrasing. This type of editing is often the last stage of editing before proofreading. We will come on to proofreading in the next chapter.

Line editing pays close attention to the mechanics of the text, such as sentence length and complexity, rhythm, and clarity. The editor will make suggestions for revisions that can help improve the flow and coherence of the text and make it more engaging and easy to read.

Content Editing

A type of editing that focuses on the quality of the writing. The aim is to help the author refine and improve the writing, making it concise, clear, and engaging.

A content editor will review the manuscript line by line, focusing on writing style, tone, voice, and the story's details. The editor will suggest improvements, such as clarifying unclear passages, eliminating redundancies, and enhancing character development. Additionally, they will provide feedback on pacing, dialogue, and the flow of the story.

This type of editing is essential for authors who aim to elevate their writing and ensure their book is clear, concise, and engaging. Content editing helps identify and address any weaknesses in the manuscript, improving its overall coherence and structure.

Copy Editing

A type of editing that focuses on the mechanics and technical aspects of writing. The aim is to ensure that a manuscript is error-free and has consistent grammar, correct spelling and punctuation, and style.

A copy editor will review the manuscript line by line, looking for grammatical and spelling errors, awkward phrasing, and inconsistencies in style and formatting. A well-edited book is free of errors and inconsistencies, making it easier to read and understand.

Ensuring Your Editor has a Clear Understanding of Your Book

When providing information to an editor about your book, offer a comprehensive overview to ensure they understand the project's scope and requirements. Some information to include:

- Specify the target audience and the age group.
- Provide the total word count or approximate page count of your manuscript.

- Include a summary of your book, its main plot points, central themes, and characters.
- Communicate your timeline and any specific deadlines you need to meet, including the desired turnaround time for editing.
- Share any preferences or guidelines regarding writing style, tone, and voice.
- Provide special instructions or considerations relevant to your book, such as formatting requirements, language preferences, or specific terminology.

Completing this for a picture book should not take long.

By providing thorough and detailed information about your book, you enable the editor to tailor their approach to meet your specific needs and goals.

The Benefits of Hiring a Professional Editor for Your Manuscript

Following the editing process you'll receive a version of the document that highlights all changes made, allowing for easy review, along with a clean copy.

Hiring a professional editor brings an objective and experienced perspective to your work, offering insights and suggestions to enhance its quality. They possess the expertise to identify and rectify issues related to plot structure, character development, and overall coherence, ensuring your manuscript reaches its full potential. Additionally, a professional editor ensures that your writing adheres to grammar and style conventions, elevating its professionalism and readability. Ultimately producing a polished book ready for proofreading. Some editors may also cover the proofreading stage too.

A picture book should not take long for this process to complete. I have found it can take up to 2-4 days.

Finding Editors Websites to Begin Your Search

There are many online sites where you can search for editors. Here are a couple to get you started:

Reedsy

Exports - Your Ultimate Guide To Writing Picture Books And Self Publishing - Reedsy

FIVERR

Fiverr - Freelance Services Marketplace

Chapter Summary

- Professional editing must be seen as a crucial stage.
- Decide which type of editing is suitable for your book.
- Supply the editor relevant details to ensure their approach aligns with your needs.

12

Proofreading

Understanding the Role of a Proofreader in Document Preparation

A proofreader is a professional who reviews written document content and corrects grammar, spelling, punctuation, and formatting. So overall, they will check that the document does not contain any mistakes before you move on to publishing the book for sale. You might be wondering how this differs from the editing process.

Proofreaders and the editing process have distinct roles.

- The editing review will address issues related to content, structure, style, and overall narrative flow to shape the manuscript. The editing process contributes to the overall, broader improvements.

- Proofreaders focus on the final stage and should meticulously examine the text for grammar, punctuation, spelling, and formatting issues. The proofreading stage should give you a polished, error-free final document.

If you hire someone to edit, they may also include proofreading.

Areas Covered by a Proofreader in Document Review

There are various areas that proofreaders will check, and the more you would like checked may add to the overall price.

Some of the areas covered by a proofreader are listed below:

- Identifying and rectifying spelling mistakes, typos, and misspellings.
- Ensuring the correct usage of grammar and sentence structure.
- Verifying the correct use of punctuation marks.
- Consistent capitalisation and proper use throughout the manuscript.
- Reviewing the overall structure of sentences and paragraphs.
- Highlighting or addressing any phrases or expressions that are a bit awkward.
- Checking font, spacing, and indentation.
- Pointing out and fixing repeated words.
- Proper use of italics, words in bold, and other areas of formatting.

- Validating that the writing adheres to a consistent style.

Following the proof reading process, you'll receive a version of the document that highlights all changes made, allowing for easy review, along with a clean copy. The role of a proofreader should be to give you a book that is error-free and ready for printing.

Websites to Begin Your Proofreader Search

There are many online sites where you can search for proof readers. Here are a couple to get you started:

Reedsy

Exports - Your Ultimate Guide To Writing Picture Books And Self Publishing - Reedsy

FIVERR

Fiverr - Freelance Services Marketplace

Chapter Summary

- Proofreading differs from editing.
- A proofreader should give you an error-free document ready for printing.

13

Choosing A Title

Tips for Choosing a Title for Your Picture Book

Choosing a title for your picture book is crucial to attracting potential buyers. I start by writing a list of all the titles I can think of for my book. I then leave the list somewhere I will see it often and slowly cross them out until one is left.

Here are some things to consider:

- Think about the central message, theme, or moral that you chose. Your title could capture the core of this.
- Consider the age group the picture book is for. The title needs to appeal to this age group.
- Try to use words that evoke curiosity, emotion, and interest. This may make potential buyers pick up your book to find out more.

- Think about tone. Is the book adventurous, educational, humorous, etc.? Try to incorporate the tone within the title to emphasis what is inside.
- Aim for a punchy, concise title while conveying the essence of the story.
- Incorporating a character starts to set expectations for the content.
- Strive for originality to make your book stand out. As a tip, try to search to see if your title or a similar one has already been used and consider a different one.
- Consider how the cover illustration may complement the title chosen.

Using Keywords Effectively in Your Book Title

Keywords are an important area to be aware of, and clever use of keywords in your title may make your book easier to find.

For example, using one of my books:

- Title: **Elephant** May's Slippery Day
- Keyword: would be **Elephant**

So, anyone searching for "Elephant" has a chance of my book appearing in the search results. For example, they might search for "Elephant picture book." Consider using words in your title that reflect the main aspects of your book and what potential buyers may use to search for a book like yours.

I could have just gone for 'May's Slippery Day.' or 'Watch out May!' However, without a keyword in the title would make the book harder to find.

You will also have the option to add a subtitle when you upload your book to a selling platform.

Taking the example earlier:

- Title: **Elephant** May's Slippery Day
- Subtitle: Come and find out how to stop an **elephant** sliding down a hill!

Both have the keyword mentioned.

The example given is a simplistic one using the word "elephant," a broad search term, to demonstrate the concept of how keywords work. Keywords are ideal to be aware of from the start as they may change or influence what you had in mind for the title of your book.

Guidelines for Creating a Picture Book Title

When creating a title for a picture book there are several elements you should avoid to ensure it resonates well with young readers and adults.

- Avoid overly long titles. Keeping the title short and easy to remember is crucial for young children.

- Use simple, child-friendly language rather than complex words that might be difficult for children to understand.
- Avoid titles that are too abstract or hard for young children to grasp.
- The title should reflect the story or theme of the book.
- Avoid unusual words and spellings.
- Keep punctuation minimal to ensure your title remains clear and straightforward to search for.

Feedback on your Book Title Idea

Once you have a book title idea, a tip would be to gain feedback from potential buyers and readers.

Here are some ideas to effectively gain and use feedback:

- Ask friends, family, and colleagues for their opinions on your book title. They can provide initial reactions and suggestions for improvement.
- Utilise platforms like Facebook, Twitter, and Instagram to conduct polls or ask for feedback.
- Participate in online forums and groups related to writing and books, such as Goodreads. These platforms can provide valuable insights from people who are passionate about books.
- Gain feedback from parents, teachers, and from children. Children's reactions are honest, and they will give great feedback.

Chapter Summary

- The title is the first impression of your picture book.
- Take your time to choose a title.
- Brainstorm all the potential titles.
- Check that the title has not been used already.
- Reflect the overall story within the title.
- Think about key words that potential buyers will use to search for your book.
- Gain feedback on your title ideas.

14

Illustrations

If you are lucky enough to be able to do your illustrations, I wish you fun bringing your book to life.

Finding the Right Illustrator for Your Picture Book

If you need to find an illustrator this is a crucial decision as the illustrations play a significant role in conveying the story and engaging with your readers.

I work with multiple illustrators, whom I found in different ways.

I used an illustrator agency website to search through the portfolios until I found the style I was after. I used Advocate Art and took the time to search through their portfolio of illustrators. When I saw an illustrator's style I was looking for, I made contact to request availability and cost. The assigned agent was extremely helpful and suggested a few other illustrators with similar styles to ensure I was choosing the one right for me. However, it was an easy decision, as no one caught my eye as much as Melanie Mitchell. Melanie has since illustrated a number of my books.

The other illustrator I use, Pei Jen, I found on social media. I looked at their portfolio and reviews and made contact to discuss working with them further. I was satisfied with their professionalism and responses and went ahead. Pei Jen has also illustrated multiple books for me.

I have been lucky as I have two amazing illustrators who are easy to work with and understand my vision. Maybe in the future I will work with more.

Take your time and make sure you are happy with the illustrator chosen and that they understand your vision. Getting this right will save you time with revisions and should make the illustrator stage an enjoyable collaboration.

Starting Your Search for an Illustrator

Here are a few suggestions to start you off looking for an illustrator. There are also social media sites as an option:

Illustration Agency | Advocate - Art

Fiverr Pro: Top freelance talent and powerful business tools

Hire Freelancers & Find Freelance Jobs Online | Freelancer

Guru.com - Find and Hire Expert Freelancers

Some of these sites will ask you to post the amount you are willing to pay (a bid value). Illustrators interested in your project will then submit bids for you to consider. Carefully review all the portfolios to see if their style suits what you are after, and once you have shortlisted a few illustrators, message them to discuss their prices and what they include. Remember to take a look at their reviews. As per the areas below, you can also request a sample of their work to ensure their style matches what you are looking for in your book and that they can interpret your instructions accurately.

Things to Consider When Choose an Illustrator

Here are a few areas to consider when deciding on an illustration style and illustrator:

- Take your time to look at other picture books to explore styles. See if you can find one or a few that are like what you have in mind. You then have an idea when you start to look at portfolios.
- Keep your vision in mind when deciding on a style.
- Research illustrators by looking at their portfolios and any recommendations they may have. You will find an

abundance of illustrators online through their websites and on social media platforms.
- Considering their experience and work history may be a factor for you. You may like to select an experienced illustrator who has experience illustrating multiple picture books.
- Ask for examples of previous projects and client testimonials.
- Usually, the more experience an illustrator has, the greater the cost.
- Set your budget and ensure that, from the start, you are aware of the complete cost. Discuss whether adjustments are unlimited for the price or whether there would be an additional cost for adjustments beyond x amount.
- It is advisable to request the agreement and terms in writing within a contract. The agreement should stipulate timelines, revisions, rights, and royalties. Covering this information is crucial to prevent any legal disputes or disagreements later on. Ensure the contract states that all rights to the illustrations are signed over to you, making you the sole holder of the rights. Being the sole holder of the rights means that once the illustrations are complete, they belong to you in their entirety. There is always the option of consulting with a legal professional who can ensure the contract protects your interests. If you choose an illustrator from a site specifically for finding illustrators, this site may take care of the agreement and terms - make sure you read these through.
- Asking for recommendations from other authors is an option. If you do not know any, reach out to the many on social media platforms; most are willing to share information.

- You can also ask the illustrator to provide a test illustration based on your book to ensure their interpretation is what you had imagined, and it gives you a peek at what they would be like to work with. Some illustrators may charge a small fee for this.

Illustration Costs to Consider

It is also worth mentioning that different sizes of illustrations come with differing costs.

These include:

- Spot images
- Half page
- Full page
- Double-page spread
- The cover usually has its own cost too.

Each of the above changes the price. If you have a book with all double-page images, this would be more expensive than having them on half-pages.

Payment Structures for Illustrators

Find out what the costs are for each up front so you can ensure the illustrator is within your budget.

Payments are usually made at specific stages (milestones) throughout a project. Typically, this includes:

- *One payment upfront*
- *One upon completion of the drafts*
- *A final payment at the end*

Advocate Art, the agency I used to find an illustrator, structured the payments this way. However, other arrangements may exist depending on the agency or individual you work with, so it's important to discuss and agree on the terms.

For example, if you use a platform like Freelancer, you would make the full payment upfront to the platform, which holds the payment. Once you are satisfied with the completed work and have signed off on it, the payment is released to the illustrator.

You may come across the terms **flat fee** and **percentage of sales**:

- **Flat Fee**: A one-time payment agreed upon before the project begins. This covers the entire cost of the illustrations, regardless of how many books you sell.
- **Percentage of Sales**: The illustrator receives a percentage of the sales revenue from the book. This is less common but might be negotiated in certain situations.

Ensure you understand and are comfortable with the payment terms before starting your project. Clear agreements help avoid misunderstandings and ensure a smooth working relationship.

Illustration Approval Process

The illustrator should provide you with rough drafts for approval before finalising them. Here is a typical workflow:

1.Rough Drafts:

- The illustrator sends you rough sketches of the illustrations.
- At this stage, you can request changes until you are happy with the drafts. The number of changes allowed should be specified in your agreement.

2.Approval of Rough Drafts:

- Once you approve the rough drafts, the illustrator will proceed to create the final versions.

3.Colour Image (if applicable):

- If your book is in colour, the illustrator will then provide coloured versions of the approved drafts.
- You may be able to request minor tweaks after receiving the coloured images, but this depends on your agreement with the illustrator.

4.Final Drafts:

- Once the coloured images are finalised and approved, these are typically considered the final illustrations.

Make sure your agreement with the illustrator includes clear terms about the number of revisions allowed and the approval process for each stage. This helps ensure a smooth collaboration and a final product that meets your expectations.

Text Placement in Illustrations

Some illustrators will place the wording on the page for you and some will provide the illustrations only. Here's what you need to consider:

Text Placement by Illustrator:

- Some illustrators include text placement as part of their service.
- This can simplify the process as the same person handles both the illustrations and text, ensuring consistency in the design.

Illustrations Only:

- Other illustrators may only provide the illustrations, requiring you to arrange for the text to be added separately.
- This might involve additional costs if you need to hire

someone else to handle the text placement.

Check Upfront:

- Discuss these details with your illustrator at the beginning of the project.
- Clarify whether they will handle text placement and if it incurs additional costs.

Both of my illustrators place the wording, as I find it easier to have the same person do both. This ensures a cohesive design and can streamline the production process.

Managing Text Placement in Your Picture Book

Deciding where the wording appears on each page of your picture book is an important step in the publishing process. Here's how I approach it:

Manual Drafting Process:

- Sometimes I create a draft book using plain paper and tape.
- I print out the wording and cut it into separate paragraphs.
- By physically moving the text around on each page, I visualise and adjust until satisfied.
- This tactile approach helps me visualise the final layout and is a personal preference.

Using Word Documents:

- Alternatively, if I'm clear on the text placement, I use a Word document.
- I organise the wording with headers indicating the page ranges (Pages 1-2, Pages 3-4, etc.).
- This method provides a structured format to communicate text placement to the illustrator.

Providing Instructions to the Illustrator:

- Ensure you convey this information clearly to your illustrator.
- If using the manual draft method, summarise the specific wording for each page in a Word document.
- Avoid sending the physical dummy book to the illustrator; instead, use your notes and instructions to guide them effectively.

By organising text placement in this way, you maintain control over the layout while ensuring clarity and consistency in your picture book project.

Communicating Your Vision to the Illustrator

When working with an illustrator for your picture book, it's essential to effectively convey your vision for the illustrations. Here are key steps I follow to ensure clarity and alignment with my expectations:

Providing Detailed Descriptions:

- Rather than leaving interpretation solely to the illustrator, I provide detailed thoughts and descriptions for each page.
- This helps ensure that the drafts align closely with my vision, reducing the need for extensive revisions.

Confirming Image Sizes and Costs:

- Specify the desired image size for each page to maintain consistency throughout the book.
- Include estimated costs for each image in your initial draft to manage your budget effectively.

Example of Notes to the Illustrator

Below is an extract from my notes for "Elephant May's Most Slippery Day," illustrating how I document my vision for each page:

In the boxes is the story text to keep this from getting muddled with my thoughts for the page. I also like to give a few images to try to pass on what I had in mind as a guide for the illustration style:

ILLUSTRATIONS

Elephant May's Slippery Day – Illustrator Notes

First page
Title page spot image

Title page and copy right text
Image – to be decided later

Page 1 and 2 (the first double page)

```
As the sun rose in the morning, starting to brighten
the day,
A long grey trunk was stirring. It belonged to
Elephant May.

She gave an excited trumpet as she pirouetted from
bed,
then hummed as she brushed her tusks and the tuft of
hair on her head.
```

Page 1

Half page image: A room with a window with a sunrise. Image of Elephant May in bed I thought she could be lying on her tummy, so there is the shape of her bum under the covers, and May is peeking out with her trunk sticking out of the covers, with arms stretched out. A little sleep hat and PJ's. A ballet dancer soft toy as a snuggly.

Page 2

Quarter page image: Elephant May looking like she is pirouetting, with her bed in the background, still holding her ballet dancer snuggly in one hand and her night hat in the other.

Quarter page image: Elephant May brushing her tufty hair while still wearing her PJ's in front of a mirror. Could you do her with the brush pulling the hair up with one hand and the other hand brushing her tusk?

Page 3 and 4

```
May two-stepped to her tutu and jumped into her
boots.
Then she grabbed her wicker basket for collecting
yummy fruits.

She set off on her journey, the one she made every
day,
practising her ballet, as she twirled along the way.
```

Page 3

Three quarter page image: May, wearing a tutu and jumping towards her boots. I thought this type of move looked quite good; see the ballet mouse picture. I think a bow in her hair would look good too, or I saw the below picture of a crown, or she could have little bows at the start of each ear. Although I am not sure if that would look odd . I quite like the gold and pink colour scheme, but I am open to your thoughts as well. I googled ballet dancer boots. Ignore the complete look of these, but can you do this type of thing with lace up fronts for little boots and a bow at the top? More dainty looking though. May's tail would need to be sticking out of a hole at the back of the dress. The big bow on the back is quite nice.

ILLUSTRATIONS

Page 4

Half page: May leaving her house with the door shut behind, holding her wicker basket in her hand in a ballerina pose with the wicker basket up in the air and twirling with a big smile. A couple of small African reptiles could be on the ground. I have seen some nice colourful lizards from South Africa, or a line of meercats perhaps looking.

FROM CONCEPT TO CREATION: YOUR ULTIMATE GUIDE TO WRITING PICTURE BOOKS AND SELF PUBLISHING

Page 5 and 6

```
Now today was slightly different. It didn't go quite
as planned,
as May didn't see a banana skin where she was about
to land.

May's heel made sudden contact with this
super-slippery fruit.
Off she skidded down the hill, with her basket in
hot pursuit.
```

Full spread: May at the top of the village hill, slipping on the banana skin. The banana skin stuck to the bottom of her ballet boot. Her basket up in the air. The idea would be that as May is slipping down the hill, there are houses and shops as she goes down. Some are selling fruit, baskets, etc. Maybe washing hanging on a line, and other things to add colour. I thought the houses on wooden stilts would work best as they are on a hill. For these pages, could there be the animals in the background with Beth Buffalo first, as she comes up in the next verse.

Page 7 and 8

```
Beth the buffalo was first to see, poor May sliding
past.
She jumped and grabbed the elephant's tail, but
found she was going too fast.
```

Page 7

Half page: Beth the buffalo, looking shocked with a bit of background. She could be outside her shop, which sells colourful cushions. Later, when the lion is napping under his tree, he could have one under his head perhaps. A lot of buffalo pictures have a bird on them too, which I think might be a nice touch.

This is the end of the example as to how I supply the illustrator my ideas.

The size of your images will also determine whether your book fits the standard thirty-two page picture book format. For example, when planning "Mr. Vole's Upside-Down New Pots" I added two extra pages, making it a 34-page picture book to maintain the story's flow and avoid overcrowding the last pages with text.

Trimming and Bleed Allowances in Book Publishing

Be sure to specify the size of your book, as the illustrator will need to account for trimming and bleed allowances.

- **Trimming** refers to the process of cutting the printed material down to its final size. Printers typically print multiple copies of a design on a larger sheet of paper, known as a parent sheet. After printing, the parent sheet is trimmed along crop marks to produce individual copies. It's essential to ensure that the design elements extend to the trim edge to avoid white borders.
- **Bleed allowance** refers to the extra space added to the design beyond the trim edge. This extra space ensures that when the parent sheet is trimmed, any slight inconsistencies or shifts in the cutting process won't leave white borders on the final product. Typically, bleed allowance is around 3 mm to 5 mm (0.125 to 0.25 inches) beyond the trim edge. This is crucial for images that cover the whole page and to ensure the cover will not be impacted.

Your illustrator may need to know where you plan to upload your book so they can refer to the measurements of these two elements from the website. If you choose to illustrate your book be aware of this and factor this into the overall design.

Provide the ISBN and Barcode to Your Illustrator

Remember to also send the illustrator the ISBN and bar code once you have registered it against the book. The ISBN and bar code are usually located on the back of the book, on the bottom right-hand side. Refer to the chapter that covers ISBN and bar codes.

Understanding the Gutter

When reviewing the illustrations for your book, it's crucial to remember the gutter—the centre margin where the pages are bound. Here's why it matters:

- The gutter is the central area where pages meet and are bound together in a book.
- Illustrations and text near the gutter can be partially obscured or difficult to view due to binding.

When reviewing the illustrations keep this in mind and ensure that critical elements of your illustrations, such as characters or key details, are not lost in the gutter. Check that important visual elements are away from the gutter to avoid them being obscured or difficult to see. Your illustrator should ensure this does not occur however it is always good to have this in mind when you view the images.

Inform the Illustrator of Any Dedications

If you are dedicating the book to someone or something, you need to inform the illustrator where to place the text along with the text.

Chapter Summary

```
- Decide on the illustration style you are after.
- Choose an illustrator who can provide this style.
- Understand the costs upfront.
- Ask about alterations and any restrictions on the
number you can make.
- Document the agreement and review the terms of the
contract.
- Give clear instructions to the illustrator.
- Make sure required trim and bleed allowances are
catered for.
- Supply the bar code and ISBN.
- Enjoy! This is such a fun stage!
```

15

The Cover

DIY vs. Hiring a Professional

Creating an eye-catching cover is crucial for your book's success. Here's why you might consider hiring a cover designer/illustrator instead of DIY:

Benefits of Hiring a Cover Designer/Illustrator:

- Professionals understand visual appeal, market trends, and design principles that attract readers.
- A well-designed cover grabs attention and communicates the essence of your book effectively.
- Professionals create unique, polished designs that differentiate your book in a crowded market.
- A compelling cover can influence purchase decisions and increase sales.

Considerations for DIY Cover Design:

- Assess your design skills honestly; a poorly designed cover may deter potential readers.
- Designing a cover requires time and effort that could be spent on writing or marketing.
- While DIY may save money upfront, a professional cover could lead to higher long-term sales.

Why First-time Authors Should Consider Hiring:

- Professionals ensure your cover aligns with industry standards and reader expectations.
- Cover designers offer insights and revisions to optimise visual impact and marketability.
- A well-designed cover enhances your book's appeal and supports future marketing efforts.

Choosing between DIY and hiring a professional depends on your skills, budget, and goals. Investing in a professional cover designer/illustrator can maximise your book's potential, ensuring it stands out in a competitive market and attracts your target audience effectively.

Guiding Your Front Cover Design

For the front cover the author usually steers the overall elements. Therefore, you will probably need to provide input on whether characters are to be on the front cover, the scene, and what you feel best represents the book. This will give the illustrator clear guidance to ensure they create what you have in mind. While some illustrators might be comfortable drafting without specific instructions, in my experience, it is beneficial for the author to provide their ideas. This helps the illustrator better align their work with your vision

Utilising Amazon to Explore Picture Book Styles

When searching on Amazon for picture book styles you are not only gaining inspiration but also setting a foundation for discussions with your illustrator. Here's how to effectively use this approach:

Exploration and Inspiration

- Browse through a variety of picture books available on Amazon. Look for titles that resonate with your story's tone, themes, and target audience.
- Pay attention to illustrations that appeal to you. Note the artistic style, use of colours, and how characters and scenes are depicted.
- Look at the book's layout using the often available look inside feature. Review how text is integrated with the illustrations, the page composition, and overall visual storytelling.

Communicating with Your Illustrator

- Select a few picture books that closely align with your vision. Highlight specific elements you admire, such as art style, character expressions, or the way scenes are portrayed.
- Provide these books as reference materials to your illustrator. This helps them understand the aesthetic and design preferences you envision for your own book.
- Use these examples as a starting point for discussions. Discuss what aspects you like and how they might be adapted to fit your narrative.

Facilitating Collaboration

- Ensure your illustrator understands that these examples are for inspiration and guidance rather than to copy.
- Encourage a collaborative process where your illustrator can share initial sketches or concepts based on the discussed styles. Provide feedback to refine and align the visuals with your vision.
- Remain open to creative interpretations and suggestions from the illustrator. Their expertise can enrich the visual storytelling of your book.

Incorporating Sketches into the Illustration Process

Utilising sketches can significantly enhance the collaboration with your illustrator. Here's how you can effectively integrate your sketches into the illustration process:

Sketching Process

- Start by sketching out your ideas with a pencil. These rough sketches serve as a preliminary visual representation of your vision for the illustrations.
- Refine your sketches until you are satisfied with the composition, characters, and overall layout. This iterative approach allows you to explore different possibilities before finalising your concepts.
- Use your sketches to communicate specific details such as character designs, scene compositions, and key visual elements. This visual guidance helps the illustrator understand your preferences more clearly.

Collaborating with Your Illustrator

- Share your finalised sketches with the illustrator. Explain that these sketches are intended to serve as a foundation or inspiration for their mock-ups.
- Alternatively, if you prefer not to sketch, write a few paragraphs detailing your visual ideas and expectations. This narrative approach can also effectively convey your

vision.
- Engage in discussions with the illustrator about how they interpret your sketches or written descriptions. Encourage them to provide feedback and suggestions to further refine the illustrations.

Remember that the cover includes both the front and back covers. So, you will need to draft out both.

Designing a Front Cover Wrap-around Illustration

I went for a front cover that wraps around the back, so one scene covers the front and back of the book. You could, however, have a different type of cover where the picture on the front is different from the one on the back. Look at a few picture books to see if this triggers the style you would like and what you feel will work best for the cover to portray the content of your book. I have left the spine blank, the picture from the front wraps around so you see a small part of the illustration on the spine. Some sites that you upload to will recommend that you leave the spine blank.

Crafting an Engaging Picture Book Cover

It is then up to the illustrator to translate your vision into an appealing cover. While I have mentioned illustrators there is also the option of exploring book cover designers. However, many illustrators are also adept at designing covers. The benefit of using the same illustrator is that they can maintain consistency with the content and incorporate characters and other features from the book. A book cover designer might be useful if you are seeking design ideas but not necessarily hiring them to illustrate them. I will therefore keep referring to Illustrator throughout this section.

The cover design is often an iterative process. The author provides feedback on the drafts, and the illustrator makes revisions until the cover is agreed upon. The number of revisions should be discussed before the work commences, along with the cost.

You need to ensure that the front cover reflects the content of the picture book and grabs the attention of the target audience and adults who will be purchasing the book. The picture book market is incredibly competitive, so try to make yours stand out. Remember that your cover should attract both children and adults.

A few areas to consider:

- Your book cover needs to draw the person looking at it into the story and make them open the book to discover more.
- Ensure your cover has appealing colours. Younger people tend to be drawn to bright, joyful colours. However, as ages increase, this may start to change, and colour schemes can start to be more complex.
- Think about how intricate the illustrations are. Younger children may be drawn to more minimalist looks.

- Consider the size of your font. Bigger text may be more appealing to the age group of picture books.
- It is also important to not use a font that is overly complex and harder to read. Although children may not be able to read when they first receive your book, they will progress to this stage.
- Title length also needs to be thought about. A short one and easy to read vs. a longer one but a catchy one that can be remembered.
- Try to capture the atmosphere of the book: adventurous, humorous, to name a couple.

Engaging Your Audience in Cover Design

When finalising your picture book cover consider involving your audience to gain valuable feedback and generate interest. Here are some strategies to maximise engagement and ensure your cover resonates with readers:

Seek Feedback on Social Media

- Share your cover ideas on social media platforms like Facebook, Instagram, or Twitter. Invite your followers and fellow authors to provide comments and feedback. This can offer diverse perspectives and insights.
- Engage directly with your audience by posting polls or questions about different cover options. This interactive approach can generate excitement and anticipation for

your book.

Involving Local Schools

- Partner with a local school to showcase your cover to students within your target age group. Their responses can provide authentic feedback on what attracts young readers and help refine your design.
- Consider offering a free book reading or author visit to the school once your book is published.

Tips for Gathering Feedback

- Provide clear instructions when seeking feedback. Encourage specific comments on design elements, colours, and overall appeal.
- Use feedback to gauge initial reactions and identify potential areas for improvement. Balance personal preferences with audience expectations to ensure broad appeal.

Crafting a Compelling Back Cover for Your Picture Book

The back cover of your picture book is a critical component for enticing potential readers and connecting with them. Here's how you can effectively utilise this space to enhance your book's appeal and engagement:

Synopsis of the Book

- The back cover serves as a snapshot of your book's essence. Craft a concise summary, approximately 250 words, that encapsulates the main themes, characters, and plot without revealing too much. This summary should intrigue readers and compel them to purchase the book to delve into the story.

About the Author

- Consider including an 'About the Author' section to establish a personal connection with readers. Share brief insights into your background, inspiration for writing, or any relevant experiences that influenced your book. A photo can also humanise your author persona and foster a sense of familiarity.

Calls to Action

- Incorporate calls to action strategically to encourage reader engagement. Examples include inviting readers to leave a review, visit your website or social media profiles, or subscribe to updates. This prompts active participation and strengthens reader-author relationships.

Finalising Your Book Cover

The cover is a fun stage but take your time and make sure you are completely happy with it. Here's how to navigate this crucial stage with care and attention to detail:

Quality Assurance

- Take the time to thoroughly review both the front and back covers. Ensure all elements, including illustrations, text placement, and colour schemes, align with your vision and effectively convey the book's essence.
- If needed, provide constructive feedback to your illustrator or designer for any necessary adjustments. This ensures the final cover reflects your expectations and resonates with your target audience.

Reviewing the Entire Package

- Once satisfied with the cover, review it in conjunction with the completed interior pages of your book. Check for consistency in design elements, font styles, and overall presentation to maintain a cohesive visual identity.

After confirming all revisions and adjustments, give your approval for the finalised cover.

Securing Your Completed Book

After completing the pages and cover of your picture book it's crucial to safeguard your work for future reference and protection. Here's how to ensure your final product is securely stored:

Choosing the Right Format

- Obtain the final version of your book from your illustrator or book cover designer in the agreed-upon format, suitable for both digital and print purposes.
- Save your book files to multiple locations.

Organising and Archiving

- Archive all background ideas, drafts, and working files, dated for reference and historical tracking. This documentation provides insight into your creative process and aids in future revisions or adaptations.

Security and Accessibility

- I store files on an external hard drive.
- I utilise cloud services for convenient access from anywhere and additional protection.

Maintaining Version Control

- Implement version control practices to manage changes

and updates effectively. Label and organise files with clear naming conventions to distinguish between drafts and final versions.

By securing your completed picture book in multiple formats and storing all related materials systematically you safeguard your creative efforts, and ensure accessibility for future.

Chapter Summary

```
- The cover is the first impression of your book,
make yours stand out.
- Take advantage of the many free apps online that
can assist with book cover design and ideas.
- Think about what would best reflect the content of
your book, the message, morale or theme.
- You need a cover that appeals to children as well
as adults.
- Guide the illustrator with sketches, or a few
paragraphs, on any ideas you may have of what to
include on the cover.
- Save everything along with the drafts and any
background documents.
```

16

ISBN and Bar Codes

As you are approaching your picture book being documented and illustrated, and should you decide to go down the self-publishing route and would like your book to be a printed book, then you will need to purchase an ISBN. Printed books cannot be sold without an ISBN. For each format of your book, you will require an ISBN For example hard cover/soft cover. Digital books such as e-books do not always require an ISBN. Check the platform you choose to see whether this is the case. For example, when publishing through Amazon KDP, Amazon assigns you a 10-digit Amazon Standard Identification Number (ASIN).

What is an ISBN?

- ISBN stands for International Standard Book Number.
- It is a unique 13-digit product number (before 2007, 10 dig-

its were used) used by bookshops, libraries, and publishers for ordering, listing, and stock control. It enables them to identify particular publishers.
- Each part of the 13-digit number has a purpose:
- A prefix element (3 digits), which currently can only be 978 or 979.
- A registration group element (1-5 digits), that identifies the nation or geographical region of a publication.
- A registrant element (7 digits or fewer), denotes the specific publisher or imprint of the text.
- A publication element (6 digits or fewer), which identifies the specific edition of a title (1st edition, 2nd edition, paperback edition, digital edition, special edition, etc.).
- A check digit (1 digit), which mathematically validates the rest of the number.
- An ISBN identifies the title of the book as well as the edition and format.
- Suppliers of the book will use the ISBN to identify which books are on their records which assist them with ordering. These include bookshops, libraries, and online retailers to name a few.
- You will usually see the ISBN on the back of books in the bottom right-hand corner. If it is not located there, then it will be located with the copyright text and publisher information.
- It is worth mentioning that as the ISBN is unique per book, if, in the future, you decide to reprint or republish your book, then you will need to allocate a new ISBN.

What is a Barcode?

- Barcodes are distinct identification codes used to uniquely identify your book and enable point-of-sale transactions. It encodes information, including the ISBN, for easy scanning. A barcode usually consists of black bars and white spaces, and these are located on the back of the book alongside the ISBN or with the copyright text and publisher information as mentioned earlier.

An example of an ISBN and Barcode

Understanding ISBN and Barcode Costs for Self-Publishing

When you purchase the ISBN and bar codes, you receive full instructions on what to do. Once you have chosen where to purchase them from you usually need to set-up an account. I decided to use Nielsen UK ISBN Store.

ISBNs are instantly received when ordering online after your application has been processed.

When ordering ISBNs, consider how many you will need. If you are going to publish a soft and hard copy of your book each one will need its own ISBN. If you then add an audiobook, you will need an additional ISBN.

Once you have purchased your ISBN, it is yours forever; it does not expire.

Understanding the Importance of ISBNs in Publishing

It is worth mentioning that an ISBN is not a legal requirement in the UK and Ireland. Putting it in simple terms, it is a product identification number. However, if you wish to sell your book through major book-selling chains, bookshops, or online sellers, they will require you to have an ISBN.

Managing ISBNs and Barcodes for Your Books

Once you have your ISBN and barcodes, you can manage which ones are assigned to which book through Nielson's title editor. You need to register to use this, which is free.

Once you have registered you need to add your books and assign the ISBN to the book. To add the book to Nielson's title editor, I use the easy-add book option. To start, you need to add the 13-digit ISBN, then work through the sections. Once you have added your book to Nielson's title editor, your book is then visible to book shops, libraries, and their websites in over 100 countries.

I keep an Excel spreadsheet with a list of the ISBNs and add the book title against each one so you have an easy reference to refer to. You can easily do this in Word or write it down if you prefer. If you plan to publish multiple books, it will save you time having them recorded somewhere.

Considerations of Choosing Between Free and Purchased ISBNs

When you upload your book to online selling platforms, you may get the option for them to assign an ISBN for free. Make sure you investigate the pros and cons of going with the free ISBN.

I decided against this as, looking into this, these were the three areas flagged:

- Having your own ISBN leaves you in control of your meta data (book info) so things like book descriptions and categories for book discoverability are in your control.
- If you have your own ISBN, you will be the publisher. If you receive the free ISBN, that company will be the publisher. Having someone else be the publisher may reduce the number of outlets selling your book.
- You may not be able to use the free ISBN outside of that retail platform and any expanded distribution channels they may have.

If you are considering the free ISBN then do your research to make sure this option best suits what you are setting out to achieve.

Chapter Summary

- Look into the pros and cons of purchased ISBN and barcodes vs. free ones.
- To sell books, you will require an ISBN.
- Different formats of the book will require their own ISBN.
- The ISBN identifies key information about the book.
- Once you purchase the ISBN, this is yours forever.
- New editions of the book will require their own ISBN.

17

Comparing Online Retailers

It's essential to invest time comparing different online retailers to find the best fit for your needs. Here are some key considerations and steps you might take:

A Guide to Choosing the Right Online Platform

As an author eager to sell my books online selecting the ideal platform is crucial. The steps I took to navigate this decision:

Identifying My Needs:

Firstly, I clarified my requirements from an online platform. I considered factors such as pricing flexibility, shipping options, customer service reliability, and user-friendly interface.

Researching Online Platforms:

I explored various platforms specialising in book sales, including Amazon, Lulu, Shopify and IngramSpark. Each platform offers unique advantages and services.

Comparing Pricing and Services:

I compared the pricing structures on each platform. This included base prices, potential discounts, shipping costs, and any additional fees involved.

Evaluating Shipping Options:

I assessed the speed of delivery, international shipping availability, and associated costs to ensure my books reach readers efficiently.

Reviewing Customer Feedback:

Customer reviews provided valuable insights into each platform's performance. I paid particular attention to feedback regarding customer service, delivery times, and overall satisfaction.

Understanding Return Policies:

I reviewed the return policies of each platform to prepare for any potential need to return or exchange books, ensuring they aligned with my expectations.

Exploring Promotions and Support:

I researched ongoing promotions, discounts, and loyalty programs offered by each platform.

After thorough evaluation, I selected IngramSpark for its Print-on-Demand (POD) service and extensive global distribution network, selling books to a large number of outlets across countries. This platform allows me control over book design, pricing, and distribution options, with high-quality printing options and excellent customer support.

They provide the following:

- Print-on-demand (POD) service means that books are produced individually as orders are placed, rather than in large quantities in advance.
- Has vast distribution network. It makes printed books available to retailers, book stores, and libraries globally.
- In addition to hard and soft-cover books, they can also offer ebook distribution.
- Authors have control over the book design, upload, pricing, and distribution options.
- You can order a stock of your books through your account. I have always found this to be of high quality.
- There are support pages with frequent questions and a contactable support service if required.

There is a small fee to upload your book, however, look out for special offers. I have also seen occasions when it is free to upload on their site too. This changes all the time so refer to their website for up-to-date info.

IngramSpark: Self-Publishing Book Company | Print & Distribute

Guidelines for Uploading Books on IngramSpark

To successfully upload your book, your book file needs to be a certain size and format. Ingram Spark's website has guidance on what this needs to be. This includes things like:

- File formats: Typically, this is a PDF. Check your chosen online publishing company's website for confirmation and the latest info on Ingram Sparks should you choose this provider.
- Resolution and colour mode: There are minimum resolution sizes and colour modes.
- File size: Large files may take longer to upload and process.
- Trim size and bleed: You need to ensure the interior and cover files match the chosen trim size.

What is the Trim Size?

Trim size refers to the final dimensions of a printed book after it has been bound and trimmed. In other words, it is the size of the pages in the finished book. When you choose a trim size for your book, you are determining how large or small the physical book will be.

Accounting for Bleed

Bleed needs to be accounted for if your design extends to the edge of the book. The purpose of a bleed is to ensure that when a book is trimmed and cut to its final size, there are no white borders or unfinished edges.

Page Formatting

Some illustrators offer to format the pages of your book according to the specific requirements, making them ready for you to upload directly. Others might provide the completed separate pages, cover, and title pages, leaving the formatting to you. In this case you can either format them yourself, or hire someone else to handle the formatting. This flexibility allows you to choose the best option based on your skills, time, and budget.

If the illustrator does not provide formatting as part of their service you can hire someone to complete this, or learn how to do it yourself. I decided to hire someone, which was faster than I could achieve on my own with the time I had available. You will receive the interior file formatted for both softcover and hard cover if you choose to produce both versions, and the front covers will be provided separately. Additionally, if you decide to offer an ebook you will need a different file format specifically for that version.

I found the person I use to format my books on Fiverr. I am not affiliated in anyway however I am happy to share who I use:

Manuel G | Profile | Fiverr

Alternatively, you can purchase your own software to learn how to format the book yourself, or you may know how to do this already. I found the software expensive for the use I would get from it, which was another reason I hired someone to format the books for me. Do a search as things change and their might be free formatting tools available.

Benefits of Uploading eBook and Print Book Simultaneously

Consider uploading your eBook while you wait for your print book to be ready. After this, you will also need to wait for the proof copy to arrive to check it over before you proceed to make the print book available for purchase. It makes sense to work on uploading both formats simultaneously and launch together.

Chapter Summary

- Compare online retailers to decide which one you would like to use.
- The online retailer will have their own requirements for uploading the books on to their website.
- You can either format the book yourself, hire someone, or find an illustrator who will provide the formatted book as part of the service.

18

Uploading Your Files for a Printed Book

Once you have the files in the required format, if you haven't done so already, create an account for your chosen online publishing company.

After looking at options, I choose IngramSpark.

IngramSpark: Self-Publishing Book Company | Print & Distribute

IngramSpark is a popular platform for independent authors and publishers, offering a range of services from printing to global distribution. The platform also provides tools for managing print and digital formats, making it easier for authors to reach a broader audience.

Setting Up Your Account

The first step was to complete the information on the appropriate sign-up page. I am sure all platforms are similar if you choose a different platform.

Once you have set up your account, log into your account.

Uploading Your Book A Step-by-Step Guide

There will be various sections to complete to upload your book. I will run you through the sections.

You can save what you have entered as you go along, so you do not have to complete this all at once. You can also view and edit at any point.

To start adding a new book to the system, click "Add a Title".

You will be presented with three options:

- Print & Ebook
- Print Book Only
- Ebook Only

For this example, I have selected "print book only".

You will then be asked whether the files are ready to upload.

Select "Yes, all my files are ready".

You will then be asked to confirm that the print jacket (the cover) and print interior files are ready.

You will then have another two options:

- Print, distribute, and sell book
- Only print book

I have always selected the "print, distribute, and sell book" option with IngramSpark. This option utilises their global distribution network and print-on-demand benefits.

Next, you will need to enter the details about your book, known as metadata.

Tip: When you upload various formats of your book, you need to ensure they link on Amazon. If all your metadata matches, this should be done automatically for you. However, if they do not link, you will need to check all your metadata to see if anything does not match between the various book format descriptions and align them.

If the books still do not link you may need to contact Amazon to request that they link them for you. Below is an example of how your book should look on Amazon when all the book formats are linked. If your book is showing separately for each format this indicates the book formats are not linked.

UPLOADING YOUR FILES FOR A PRINTED BOOK

Trudy Davidson and 1 more
Lucy Lamb's Most Curious Adventure: A farm adventure about being brave and meeting new friends. (Lucy Lamb's Adventures)

Kindle Edition **USD 0.00** kindle unlimited or USD 3.81 to buy	Audiobook **USD 0.00** for membership
Hardcover **USD 9.19** ✓prime	Paperback **USD 8.92**

See all formats >

Let us look at the next section which is about title information.

- Add the title.
- Add the language the book will be published in.

- Enter the ISBN.
- You will need to confirm that you own the publishing rights or whether it is a public domain work. There is a help prompt for this and I have included an explanation below.

Owning the Publishing Rights

If you wrote the book or legally acquired the rights to publish it, you need to affirm that you hold the copyright. This ensures that you are the legal owner of the content and have the authority to publish and distribute it.

Public Domain Work

Public domain work is unprotected by intellectual property law, meaning these works cannot be owned and are free for anyone to use, adapt, reproduce, or distribute for both commercial and non-commercial purposes.

Creative works fall into the public domain for various reasons:

- The work was created before intellectual property laws existed.
- The duration of legal protection can expire, making the work public domain.
- The work is not eligible for copyright protection and enters the public domain immediately, such as mathematical formulas.

In IngramSpark, there's a drop-down section for additional book details. This section includes a subtitle, series name, series number, and edition number. Complete these fields as applicable, or remember you can update this section later if you plan to publish a series or future editions of your book.

- The next part will ask you to complete the authors and contributors information. Use the drop-down menu to select the relevant ones for your book.
- I was always recommended to complete the biography section, as this is displayed on some of the other distribution channels. Try to use the same biography as the one used on the Author Central page on Amazon. Author central is covered in a later section. This way, they stay consistent.
- Once you have more books, you can enter them into the prior work section.
- Add any affiliations that are applicable.

The following section is important to understand, and when I uploaded my first book, I did not realise why. This section will ask you to select your subjects, known as BISAC (Book Industry Standards and Communications) codes.

These codes play a crucial role in several ways:

1. BISAC codes help categorise your book's content, genre, and subject matter. This categorisation enhances the discoverability of your book, making it easier for buyers, retailers, and libraries to find titles that match their interests.
2. For online retail platforms, accurate BISAC codes ensure

your book appears in the correct categories. Using the correct categories increases the likelihood of potential buyers finding your book when searching for specific subjects.
3. If your book ends up in book stores and libraries, the book stores and libraries use BISAC codes to catalogue the books into the correct section.

These are just a few examples of the benefits of using BISAC codes. The key takeaway is that selecting the relevant subjects is essential for your book to be categorised correctly, improving its visibility and accessibility.

I came across Publisher Rocket, which has a fantastic category search facility. You pay a one-off fee to use it as frequently as you like for life. There are also many other topics covered by Publisher Rocket; this is just one of them.

The Publisher Rocket Category Feature enables you to quickly find relevant niche categories for your books. This tool helps authors identify specific categories on platforms like Amazon, where their books are more likely to stand out. Additionally, Publisher Rocket provides insights into how many books you need to aim to sell in a day to achieve the #1 bestseller rank in those categories.

With this feature, you will discover:

- Niche categories that fit your book.
- The categories that will help you sell more books.
- An idea of how many sales you may need to make the top

10.

If you would like to know more, look at this link:
Publisher Rocket | Optimize Your Book's Amazon Success
https://publisherrocket.com/?affiliate=tdavidson

Let us carry on looking at the book data to enter:

- Select which audience applies to your book.
- If a regional subject applies, complete this box.
- Thema subjects offer global and unique subjects to categorise your book.
- You then have a table of contents. A table of contents usually does not apply to a picture book.
- Once you have received review quotes, pop them in the review quote box.
- Full description box, add appropriate text for people to discover your book. Potential buyers will see this text. Try to use keywords that you will use in the keyword section within your description, as this will support your book's discoverability. Bold some of the words that you would like to stand out. Look at a few other descriptions online for books to give you some ideas of formats.

The key word section is next. Remember to use key words from your description.

- Keywords are important. I have covered them in a separate

chapter. There are various tools to help you choose keywords. Chosen online publishing companies have a tool to assist with this. Pick the most important keywords that match your book and give it the most visibility.
- You can enter up to 7 keywords and phrases.
- Remember to add a comma after each keyword or phrase to separate them.
- Enter the book's description. You have 4,000 characters to write a compelling synopsis. Focus on the story or content and highlight why readers should buy the book. If needed, consider hiring someone to write this for you. I write my descriptions, and although summarising within the recommended character count can be tricky, it is worth the effort.

The next section covers print information.

- **Trim Size**: The trim size is another way of saying what size your book should be after it has been printed. You would have decided on this at an earlier stage.
- **Interior Colour and Paper**: Here you will select if you would like your print book to be in black and white or colour. If you select black and white, you will have the option of white or crème paper. If selecting colour, you will have the option to choose between four colour interior options. I have always chosen Colour/Colour 70.
- **Binding Type**: Select whether this book is to be a hard cover or a soft cover.
- **Cover Finish:** Personal preference: whether you would like a matte or glossy cover. Look at other picture books as a

- guide and choose your preference. You can always change this option later. I chose glossy covers after ordering both to compare.
- **Page Count**: This is the total number of pages in your interior file (including blank pages, so any blank end pages).
- **ISBN**: Enter the ISBN number.
- **SKU**: If you do not want to purchase an ISBN, you may use a SKU instead. It is important to keep in mind that SKUs are not accepted in the distribution channels, so distributors will not be able to stock or sell your book if it has an SKU instead of an ISBN. I have not covered SKU in this book as I chose the ISBN route.

You are nearly there! The next section is print pricing.

For IngramSpark there are six different markets listed. Decide if you would like your book listed on all or some, and complete the pricing information. Having your book listed on all of these will make use of the global distribution, however, you may have reasons not to sell in all of them.

Online publishing companies have online calculators to help you work out what your compensation will be (how much you will get per sale). This part is over to you to decide how much you will list your book for. Your list price needs to be competitive against comparable-sized picture books.

How Much Should My Book Cost? Tips for Pricing Your Book | IngramSpark

The whole sale discount is again your choice. Read through your chosen online publishing companies' guidance. It is usually recommended to have this set at 55% for the following reasons:

- The 55% wholesale discount is commonly used in the publishing industry. It ensures that book stores and other retailers can buy books at a price that allows them to sell at a profit while covering their own expenses.
- Setting the discount at 55% makes your book more attractive to retailers. It aligns with what they expect and makes it easier for them to stock your book alongside others from larger publishers who offer similar terms.
- Many online and physical book stores, as well as distribution companies, expect a standard discount of around 55%. It can be a requirement for getting your book listed with major distributors.

The whole sale discount is how much a wholesaler will pay for your book. When the wholesaler then sells your book, a portion of this discount is passed on. The wholesaler will sell the book at the list price. This is how they profit from the book sale.

The return status needs to be completed. I set mine at Yes-Destroy. Which means the book can be returned and will be destroyed. Read your chosen online publishing companies' guidance for the options available and decide on the right one for you. I decided on making mine returnable, as it mentions that having it set to non-returnable may put people off making the order.

Always enable the look inside feature. This will let the potential buyer see the first few pages of your book.

The next stage is to upload your files.

As mentioned, although this covers IngramSpark, the information you have entered will be pretty much the same on other platforms.

After Uploading Your Book

The online publishing company will then review and approve the files. This can take a few days. You will receive notification when this has been done and your proof file is ready for review.

You will need to check over this file before you confirm it is okay for distribution. Take your time to review this. At the beginning of the print file for the online publishing company I chose, there are recommended areas for you to review, but I am sure you will check all aspects anyway.

If anything is not right, then you will need to correct your files, re-upload, and check the example print file again.

Once you are satisfied, it will print perfectly. You will receive two options: enable for distribution or choose to enable but not for distribution. I would always select enable, but not for distribution. This will allow you to order your own copy of each format you have chosen to upload.

Order and review a copy of the printed book before you enable it to be ordered by buyers. This lets you check that the book appears as it should and that the print quality meets your expectations. To date, I have had no issues with the print quality of IngramSpark.

Once you receive your copy or copies and are satisfied, everything is okay. Go back and enable distribution. You can order your own prints directly with IngramSpark to fulfil website orders, or look for other alternative printers for your own printed stock. Should you wish to hold any.

But wait for one important step.

Relish the feeling of receiving your book. Your book is finally printed and in your hands It is exciting and rewarding, and I am sure it will make you smile and maybe even cry! Shout about it, share it, and tell everyone! Be proud of this, as it has taken a lot of work and time to get that idea crafted into a picture book. Enjoy it!

Once your file has been approved it will be available to buy.

You have done it! Congratulations! Your picture book is now available globally (if you chose global distribution).

Chapter Summary

- Research and select a selling platform for your book.
- Set up an account with the selected online publishing company.
- Thoroughly complete all necessary sections for uploading your book, ensuring the accuracy and significance of the entered data and selected options.
- Keep all data the same for the different book formats so they automatically link together.
- Consider utilising websites for information to assist in key selections, such as categories.
- Activate the 'look inside' feature.
- Carefully review the proof for accuracy.
- Order your own copy of your book for your initial review.
- Savour the excitement of receiving your first copy!

19

Uploading your files (e-book)

Once you have your files formatted correctly, as discussed in the previous chapter covering printed books, the next step is to create an account on the platform where your eBook will be sold.

Choosing Different Platforms for eBooks and Printed Books

Many authors, like myself, choose a hybrid approach. For instance, I decided to distribute my hard cover and softcover books through one online publishing company and my eBooks through another.

After researching various platforms I found that using the two most popular online publishing companies for different book formats could potentially maximise exposure for my book.

Therefore, I opted to upload my eBooks to KDP (Kindle Direct Publishing) and my printed books to IngramSpark.

This approach allows me to utilise each platform's strengths for different formats while ensuring broad availability and visibility for my book across both print and digital markets.

KDP stands for Kindle Direct Publishing, a self-publishing platform by Amazon. It allows authors and publishers to independently publish and distribute their books in digital and print formats.

My books would then benefit from Amazon's online visibility, but I would also benefit from IngramSpark worldwide distribution channels. Complete your research on what is best for you. Both platforms are easy to use.

Exploring eBooks for Picture Books

I was initially unsure about offering an eBook version of my picture books. However, after completing research, I discovered that reading eBooks to children has been increasing in popularity.

Given the potential increase in usage and the simplicity of providing this format, I decided it made sense to offer an additional option for readers who might prefer it. I was also pleasantly surprised by the number of eBooks that have sold.

I also discovered that having eBooks offers several advantages.

It's an excellent way to promote your book and request reviews. Giving away eBooks during promotions is significantly more cost-effective than sending physical copies. Additionally, eBooks are easy to submit for book competitions.

Setting Up Your Account

To use KDP, you need to first sign up and create an account.

Uploading Your Book A Step-by-Step Guide

Once you have signed up,

- Go to your bookshelf.
- Click the "+ Create" button.
- Click to choose which type of book to create from the options presented.
- Enter the book title and subtitle, if relevant, as they appear on the cover.
- If the book is part of a series, enter it here, but as this is your first book, this would be left blank. If you do create a series, remember to go back and enter it here.
- Enter the author's details.
- Note any contributors. For example, the illustrator.
- Enter the book's description.
- Select the correct publishing rights option. It will almost always be "I own the copyright and I hold necessary publishing rights".
- Enter the keywords into each of the 7 available boxes.

Keywords are particularly important and covered in their own chapter. There are various tools to help you choose keywords. Pick the most important keywords that match your book to give it the most visibility. Try to think of phrases that people may enter when searching for a book like yours.
- Enter the primary marketplace where you will be selling your e-book.
- KDP allows you to select two categories for your book. Choosing the right categories is essential for increasing your book's visibility on Amazon. When readers browse categories, your book needs to appear in the appropriate ones to reach the right audience. There are tools available to help you select the most suitable categories. Placing your book in a relevant niche category can reduce competition, making it more likely for your book to be seen. Amazon's rankings are influenced by book sales within the chosen category. If you select a category with 100,000 books, you'll need to sell a significant number of copies to rise in the rankings. As a tip, search for books similar to yours on Amazon and review the categories they are listed in.
- Enter the age range of the book.
- Click 'save and continue' if you are ready to go to the next step, or 'save as draft' if you would like to come back to it later.
- The next page is where you upload your book.
- Once everything is uploaded, you will need to preview the files to make sure there are no errors or issues.
- Then the final stage is adding your pricing.

Category Search Assistance

Publisher Rocket can assist with category searches to give you this information. Use the below link details to find out more:

Publisher Rocket | Optimize Your Book's Amazon Success
https://publisherrocket.com/?affiliate=tdavidson

Chapter Summary

- Consider whether a hybrid approach would suit your needs or whether having all your book formats in one place is preferable.
- Create an account on your chosen platform.
- Enter the required information and upload your e-book.
- Pay special attention to the categories and key words entered.
- Carefully check over the sample before proceeding to publish.

20

Keywords

The Importance of Keywords for Your Book

Keywords are crucial for a book for many reasons. Here are a few of them:

- When people are searching for books, online keywords play a vital role in helping your books discoverability. If someone searches for the topic, genre, or theme of your book, you need your book to appear.
- Keywords influence how search engines rank your book in search results. By choosing relevant keywords, you can increase the likelihood of your book appearing in search listings, again improving its visibility to potential buyers.
- By researching what terms readers commonly use when searching for books similar to yours, you can optimise your book metadata (book info) to stand out more against competitors.

- Remember to use these keywords in marketing and advertising campaigns. Using these keywords can target ads to the right audience.
- If you use the correct keywords and your book is discovered when searching for them and bought, and the keyword reflects the content, genre, or theme, it will ensure that buyers' expectations are satisfied.

A Valuable Resource for Keywords and Competitive Insights

I came across a beneficial website called Publisher Rocket, and I would have liked to have known about it at the start of my journey. It is a one-off fee and you can use it as many times as you like, with no annual or monthly fee. It covers many topics; as mentioned earlier, categories are also one of them.

Using Publisher Rocket's Keywords Feature, you will learn:

- Indicates which keywords shoppers type into Amazon.
- Estimated number of times customers type that keyword into Amazon.
- An idea of how much money the books that rank for that keyword are making.
- Number of books that are competing for that keyword.

If you are interested in knowing more, check out this link:

Publisher Rocket | Optimize Your Book's Amazon Success

https://publisherrocket.com/?affiliate=tdavidson

Chapter Summary

- Choosing the right keywords is a step towards improving visibility.
- Attracts the right audience.
- Vital for competing against other similar books.
- Utilise available tools to grow your knowledge and assist you.

21

Author Central

The Benefits of Joining Amazon Author Central

Author Central is where you can share the most up-to-date information about yourself and your books with millions of readers. It helps readers find your books all in one place and gives you useful reports. Amazon Author Central is free to join, you just need to have a book listed on Amazon.

Creating Your Amazon Author Central Account

You will need to register for an account:

Amazon Author

Once your account is activated you can then create your author profile. This is your opportunity to tell potential buyers all about you. Complete as much information as you can and upload a photo. You will then need to find your books and claim them. If your book does not appear when you search for it, contact Amazon directly. You will need to claim at least one book to activate your account.

There is a section called Author Page URL. Make sure you give your page a name here. You can then share your URL link to your page on social media.

There is also an area under reports and marketing where you can enter book recommendations for books you have read and recommend your books.

1. Select Reports + Marketing from the top option bar, and then under Connect with Readers, you will see Book Recommendations. Select "Create Recommendation".
2. You will then see 'Books by Others' and another tab that says "Books I have Written".
3. Under 'Books I Have Written', you will see the following options, and you can link one of your books to these options:

- What is your most talked-about book?
- What book do you wish more readers knew about?
- What book should readers start with?
- What is a book readers can get lost in?
- Enter each section and select the book along with a note,

which is optional. Remember to go back into this section as you add more books to your collection.
- Under 'Books by Others', you will see a similar set of questions, which you can then add books to if you so wish.
- Under reports and marketing, you will see other information that you may find of interest. Total number of followers, sales ranking, and customer reviews.

The more followers you can obtain on your Amazon Author Central account will give you another avenue of communicating with followers when you have a new release or updated information about you, which could include any events you may be involved with. It can take a few days for your account to show up on Amazon. Once you are all set up, your book on Amazon will display the link to your page for people to click on.

If you would like to look at mine for ideas, please go to:

Amazon.co.uk: Trudy Davidson: books, biography, latest update

It is also worth mentioning that under the profile section, you can see what your page will look like across the various markets. Review the details you have entered at regular intervals to ensure they remain up-to-date, and you may like to refresh photos at this point too.

Have a look around Author Central as updates can occur, and features can change. I have covered a few areas, however, you may want to have a good look around to ensure you are covering the most up-to-date features. There are also advertisements for other areas that Amazon covers that may be of interest.

Chapter Summary

```
- Once you have your book on Amazon, sign up for an
Amazon Author Central page.
- It is free to sign up.
- It shares information about you and your books in
one place.
- Claim your book titles to add them to your account.
- Refresh your information and pictures regularly.
- A link from your books on Amazon will take people
to your author's central account.
- Share your page URL to increase your followers.
```

22

Marketing

From Manuscript to Market

After countless hours of hard work, dedication, and creativity, you have successfully written and produced a book. Starting with brainstorming and drafting, then progressing to revising and editing, you've navigated the entire journey of book creation with determination and skill, finally seeing your vision come to life in print, eBook, or both.

You've poured your heart and soul into your manuscript, and now, holding the finished product in your hands you can take immense pride in what you've accomplished.

Publishing a book is no small feat. You've successfully tackled all aspects ensuring that your book meets the highest standards, and is ready to be shared with the world.

Another significant aspect of your journey now begins: selling your published picture book.

Marketing is a vast and complex topic, and this guide primarily focuses on the writing and self-publishing process. However, I'll touch on a few key areas to help kick-start your marketing efforts, drawing from insights I found valuable when embarking on my author journey. Keep in mind that marketing requires a complete guidebook of its own due to its extensive nature!

So you have managed to upload your book to an online selling platform, and you wait for the sales. Without an exceptional book marketing campaign leading up to your book's release, you might notice a decline or slowdown in sales after the initial support from friends and family. Marketing is essential for any product, including your book, as it's the key to raising awareness and letting people know your book exists. With countless books available being proactive and persistent in your marketing efforts is crucial.

Social Media Platforms

I highly recommend joining social media platforms. Like Facebook, Twitter, Instagram, and LinkedIn., if you haven't already. They provide an excellent avenue for promoting your book and potentially increasing sales. With social media you can easily share links to your book within your posts, and some platforms even offer shop features, allowing you to direct users straight to where they can purchase your book. Social media platforms are ideal for sharing updates, behind-the-scenes content, and regularly engaging with your followers.

Social media platforms can be daunting if you're new to them. Learning the ropes takes time but it's worth the effort. If you're inexperienced or just starting consider browsing online tutorials and following accounts for helpful tips. Once you're comfortable you can incorporate social media into your book marketing campaign leading up to your book's release, and as part of your ongoing marketing strategy.

Managing social media can be time-consuming, especially when you post on multiple platforms and adjust the format accordingly. Then I came across Metricool. Metricool is a social media management and analytics platform that provides tools for scheduling posts, analysing performance, and monitoring metrics across various social media platforms. It offers content scheduling, audience engagement tracking, hashtag analysis, and detailed analytics reports.

Metricool has saved me so much time. With its features, you can create social media content for all platforms simultaneously and then schedule when the content will be posted. This allows you to manage multiple pieces of content at once and schedule the same content to post at different intervals. Metricool will also inform you of the best time to post based on when your followers are online, so you can choose a time to aim to get optimal views. There is a free option and a paid option with additional features.

If you are interested in learning more about Metricool, the link is here:

https://i.mtr.cool/NETHPG

Planning a Book Launch Marketing Campaign

Planning your book marketing campaign ahead of your book launch is crucial. Here is a few ideas to get you started:

- Think of ways to create buzz about your book.
- Use social media, your website blog, email newsletters if you have an email distribution list and any local area newsletters. Think about all the different avenues that may be open to you.
- Share behind-the-scenes glimpses and updates as the book progresses.
- Create eye-catching marketing material. I pay for Canva Pro and create a lot of mine using this tool, which I find easy to use. You can use Canva for free; however, there will be limitations on what you can do.
- Create videos, book trailers, book cover countdowns, and teaser images, to name a few.
- Try to get author interviews. Many social media accounts offer interviews; some charge, but some offer them for free.
- Contact people who could review your book and investigate getting book influencers.
- Collaborate with other authors. You could investigate joint

promotions.
- You could offer pre-order exclusive deals. Maybe sign books, for example.
- Respond to comments people make on your social media, it is important to interact.
- Explore virtual events. Hosting a Q&A session, reading your book, giveaways, to name a few.
- I do a cover reveal build-up on social media, starting with a snippet of the cover and gradually showing more over a few days until the final cover is revealed.

These are just a few areas to consider, but there are plenty more examples to help you formulate a marketing campaign that suits your needs. To get started I recommend doing online searches for ideas and inspiration.

Launch Team

A book launch team is a group of dedicated individuals who help an author promote their book in the weeks and months leading up to and following its release. These team members can include friends, family, fellow authors, bloggers, social media influencers, and enthusiastic readers eager to support the author and spread the word about the book.

Benefits of a launch team include:

- Leveraging networks of multiple people helps spread awareness about the book to a much larger audience than

the author could reach alone.
- Team members can promote the book in various ways, from social media posts and blog reviews to word-of-mouth recommendations and participation in online events.
- A dedicated group of supporters can create buzz and excitement around the book, increasing engagement and anticipation among potential readers.
- Launch team members often provide early feedback and reviews, which can be invaluable for refining promotional strategies and increasing credibility.
- Requesting members of the launch team to download and review your book following your book launch will help your book ranking on Amazon. You can use your eBook and offer it for free for a limited time to encourage the networks to do this for you. Let the team members know that the review doesn't need to be long; even a sentence or two will make a difference.
- Requesting the book launch team to post a review about your book with a summary of the book on their social media will also give you further exposure.

How to Build a Launch Team

- Contact friends, family, and colleagues who will support your work.
- Connect with fellow authors and readers through social media and writing communities.
- Offer incentives such as exclusive content, signed copies, and early access to the book.
- Ask members to tag others in the request to join the launch

team.

Managing the Launch Team

- Create a private Facebook group or email list to communicate with your team.
- Regularly update the team with promotional materials, key dates, and specific tasks.
- Encourage open communication and feedback within the group.
- Thank your team members regularly for their support and efforts.
- Offer public recognition, such as shout-outs on social media.

Illustrative Sample of an Invitation to Join the Launch Team:

```
Example of a Launch Team Email:
Subject: Join My Book Launch Team for [Book Title]!
Hi [Name],
I'm thrilled to announce that my new picture book
for 4-8 year olds, [Book Title], will be released on
[release date], and I'm assembling a launch team to
help spread the word. Would you be interested in
joining?

As a launch team member, you'll get:
- An advanced review copy of the book.
- Exclusive behind-the-scenes content and updates.
- The opportunity to participate in special launch
events and giveaways.

All I ask in return is that you help promote the
```

book by:
- Sharing posts on social media.
- Leaving an honest review on Amazon and Goodreads - It will be a quick read at x number of pages.
- Talking about the book with friends and family.

If you're interested, please reply to this email, and I'll send you all the details.

Thank you so much for your support!

Best, [Your Name]

Try to keep it short and add to this to make it engaging and fun. I would also add a high level sentence about the topic. For example:

Exciting news! I'm delighted to announce the upcoming release of my new picture book, "Lucy Lamb's Most Curious Adventures," tailored for children aged 4 to 8. Get ready to embark on a captivating farm adventure alongside Lucy as she explores the wonders awaiting her. Release date October 1st, join us on this enchanting journey!

KDP Select and Verified Reviews

If you enrol your eBook in KDP Select, Amazon's exclusive program for self-published authors, you can take advantage of promotional tools like Kindle Countdown Deals and Free Book Promotions. These tools can help increase your book's visibility and attract readers. Additionally, you can use these promotions to offer your eBook for free to your launch team for reviews.

When requesting reviews, it is important to ask team members to download your book from Amazon rather than basing their reviews on any free copies you may have provided. This ensures that the reviews are recorded as verified reviews, which is a crucial metric on Amazon. Verified reviews are more influential than non-verified reviews as they indicate that the reviewer has purchased and read the book, contributing to buyer confidence and positively influencing purchase decisions. Products that have received a high number of verified reviews are more likely to be trusted by shoppers.

One invaluable piece of advice I received, which I wish I had known when I began my journey as an author, is the importance of ensuring that reviewers genuinely engage with your eBook's content. It's not merely about receiving reviews but ensuring that reviews are based on an actual reading experience. Amazon employs sophisticated algorithms to detect fraudulent or misleading reviews. One way they do this is by tracking user interactions with eBooks. If a reviewer leaves feedback without demonstrating genuine engagement with the book's content, such as skipping through pages or not spending enough time reading, Amazon may flag the review as suspicious and potentially remove it.

Additionally, discourage reviewers from stating they are friends or family members, as this may also result in the review being removed.

Launch Day

It is time to officially let the world know your book is available to purchase. To make it easy for your launch team you could supply them with social media posts to share or supply images for them to use.

Setting Posts to Public

When you share your content on social media platforms such as Facebook, Twitter, or Instagram, ensure that posts are set to "public." This setting allows your posts to be viewable by anyone, regardless of whether they are your friends, followers, or connections. By making your posts public, you maximise their visibility and reach, enabling a wider audience to engage with and share your content. Making your posts "public" encourages others to share your content with their networks. When someone shares your post, it amplifies its reach, exposing it to new audiences and increasing the likelihood of engagement, such as likes, comments, and re-posts.

Clean Links And Why They Are Important

If you provide any links to your books from Amazon, also make sure you are altering the link to the book to turn it into a "clean" link. When you search for a book on Amazon the link will include other information so Amazon can determine which account searched for the book. If you share the link (the URL) and it holds your information and you keep sharing this, it might result in Amazon removing the review.

For example, when I search for Lucy Lamb's Most Curious Adventure this is the URL that displays. Everything after "ref=" needs to be deleted before you send the link:

> *https://www.amazon.co.uk/Lucy-Lambs-Most-Curious-Adventure-ebook/dp/B09Q7YRMZF/ref=sr_1_1?crid=2XC2JC4JB8VJV&dib=eyJ2IjoiMSJ9.485rIzICAKdqLoCIh9T8-Q.vqcoEkTwF_n_EMd7zvEY_EA5Og E9ipTQwz1gC3Z5blQ&dib_tag=se&keywords=lucy+lamb%27s+most&qid=1717763093&s=digital-text&sprefix=lucy+lamb%27s+most%2Cdigital-text%2C83&sr=1-1*

To share the link to your book on Amazon go to the URL displayed at the top and delete all unnecessary information.

Once you've made your deletions, press enter to ensure the link still opens your book's page on Amazon. Then share the cleaned-up link.

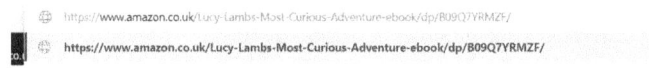

Don't be shy post, post, and post! Create regular content on social media to continue to announce your launch.

Inform your friends and family who may not be part of your launch team, especially if they do not use social media.

Join Social Media Groups

Facebook groups offer opportunities for authors to promote their books and connect with fellow writers and readers. These groups serve as vibrant communities where authors can share their work, exchange ideas, and seek support and advice from peers. By joining relevant Facebook groups, authors gain access to valuable resources, networking opportunities, and promotional channels.

There are numerous Facebook groups dedicated to book promotion and literary communities. These groups cater to various genres, niches, and interests, allowing authors to target specific audiences and engage with readers who share their passion for books. Authors can showcase their work, announce book launches or promotions, and interact with potential readers in these groups.

Search for relevant groups that might be interested in picture books. Think about parent groups, parent networks, community pages, activities for kids pages, promoting books for children, and activity groups to name a few.

You will also find groups on topics like marketing, children's picture book groups for authors, and author show off your book pages there are many more.

Creating a Website for Your Book

As part of my book marketing efforts I arranged for a website to be designed, which proved to be another valuable platform for selling my books. If you don't already have a website it's worth considering as it offers another avenue to showcase and sell your books. There are options for creating your website yourself, and you can find numerous tutorials online to help you get started.

Given my commitments to my young family, designing and building a website would require more time than I could reasonably allocate. Therefore, I opted to have my website created by a designer. The designer used a platform that allowed me to make changes myself once the website had been completed.

This way, I wasn't dependent on paying the designer for updates every time. The designer also provided helpful videos on how to handle basic tasks, which was incredibly useful. Additionally, numerous tutorials and guidance are available online, including YouTube videos, to assist with managing and updating your website.

The designer used WordPress, a website builder through Site Ground, which I find easy to use to complete further amendments. However, there are other website builders, so research and choose the one best for you. There are online demos on how to set up your website and the pros and cons of each. So far, I have found WordPress easy to navigate around, and I can work out the changes for the updates I would like to make.

Here is my website as a guide:
www.rhymingmoments.co.uk.

You can then see the sections I decided upon and the format. There are many formats, so I recommend searching for picture book websites to give you ideas for your own (not to copy). Look at the most up-to-date trends, as they tend to change frequently.

You will also need a domain name. When I began I did see articles that stated you do not need a domain name when setting up a website and there are ways around this, however, the articles also concluded it is not recommended not to have one. I did not explore this any further and opted for a domain name. A domain name varies in cost. To find out if the one you would like is available, along with the cost, you will need to search for the domain name to see whether it is in use. I use Go Daddy. I found it an extremely straightforward process with great support, and the cost was reasonable.

https://www.godaddy.com/en-uk

Utilising a blog page on your website and linking to it on social media will attempt to increase clicks to your website and may result in sales if they visit your shop.

Paying For Advertising

Look into paid advertising. There are Amazon ads and social media ads. Look at the free help on this topic online, there is loads of it. Many people charge you for courses and help with creating and managing ads, but with all the free help, I find this a waste of money. If you take time to follow the free help, you will gain the experience yourself.

Key Dates Throughout The Year

If your book has content about Easter or Christmas, ensure you are posting a few months before these dates. There are many special times and dates throughout the year, which make ideal topics to add to social media posts. To name a few:

- National Storytelling Week
- World Read Aloud Day
- World Book Day
- International Women's Day
- World Story Telling Day
- World Environment Day
- National Poetry Day
- National Non-Fiction Month

Share Received Reviews

As you begin to receive reviews about your book, it's important to share them on your social media platforms and website, along with a link for readers to purchase your book.

Attend Promotional Events

Consider participating in book fairs, author signings, literary festivals, and other events. These opportunities allow you to network with industry professionals, connect with readers, and promote your book to a wider audience. I've found attending these events to be both enjoyable and beneficial. It's rewarding to engage with people, answer their questions, and share the writing process with them.

Consider School Visits

School visits are a highlight of my author experience as they provide a wonderful opportunity to engage with young readers and share my passion for storytelling. I thoroughly enjoy preparing presentations that not only entertain but also educate children about the fascinating process of book creation. These presentations typically include interactive elements and behind-the-scenes insights into how books are made, from the initial idea to the final publication.

I adjust the level of complexity and depth of the presentation to ensure it resonates with the students and captures their interest.

- For younger children: I focus on vibrant visuals, simple language, and interactive storytelling techniques to keep them engaged and entertained.
- For older students: I delve into more detailed explanations of the writing and publishing process, encouraging critical thinking and discussion.

I have set up email distribution lists for the schools in various areas and periodically email to introduce myself and provide the benefits of author visits. I also include a brief introduction about me, the age my books are for, and a synopsis of the books along with the covers. I also add my website link.

I initially offered school visits for free before moving on to charging for them. I accept the payment as a one-off fee or I am more than happy if the school purchases books up to the fee value as it gives me more satisfaction that my books are now part of the school's library.

Before the school visit, I create a promotional code on my website for parents or adults interested in purchasing my book. Along with offering a discount, I also provide free delivery, as I bring the books to the school on the day of the visit. I typically keep the promotional code active for a month after the visit. However, if the school is local to me, I may extend the free delivery option for additional book sales, offering to drop them off in person. After the designated period, I revert the promotional code to include standard postage costs. I then provide the school with a poster to display and a one-pager to issue to the parents and adults to let them know about the visit and the discount in place should they wish to order any books. I've discovered that offering discounts through my website is more effective than providing an order sheet to the school. Aside from issuing communication about the visit and the discount, this approach eliminates all other administrative tasks for the school, which I've found is their preferred option.

My website has a page dedicated to author visits.

Author Visits - Rhyming Moments
   https://rhymingmoments.co.uk/author-visits/

These are just a few areas to explore within the vast topic of marketing. Each aspect mentioned could be further elaborated on to enhance your marketing efforts. If you decide to handle the marketing yourself, it's essential to dedicate a percentage of your time each week to these activities. Consistency, creativity, and perseverance are crucial for successfully marketing your book and maximising its reach and impact.

Chapter Summary

```
- In the run-up to your book being published, run
promotional campaigns and draft your book launch.
- If you do not already have one, consider having a
website.
- Establish profiles on key social media platforms
like Facebook, Twitter, Instagram, and LinkedIn.
Share updates, and behind-the-scenes content, and
engage with your followers regularly.
- Look at tools to help with creating social media
content. I use Canva Pro and Metricool.
- Investigate ads on the relevant platforms, and
there are also social media ads.
- Use special dates throughout the year for ideas on
marketing content.
- Consider attending book fairs, author signings,
and other events.
- Keep your metadata up-to-date. Regularly review
keywords, descriptions, and key data.
```

23

Book Awards

Book awards are prestigious honours given to exceptional literary works by various organisations, institutions, or associations. These awards recognise excellence in writing and storytelling across different genres, themes, and formats.

Benefits of Winning Book Awards

Winning or being nominated for a book award brings recognition and respect to authors and their works. It acknowledges their talent and contribution to the literary world, enhancing their reputation within the industry and among readers.

Enhancing Your Visibility with Book Awards

Book awards can boost the visibility and exposure of your book. They can attract attention within the literary community and may lead to increased book sales. Winning an award can help authors reach new audiences, expanding their readership base.

Marketing Opportunities Through Book Awards

Book awards offer valuable marketing opportunities for authors and publishers. Winning or being shortlisted for an award can be used in promotional materials to attract readers and literary professionals.

Submission Fees and Discounts for Book Awards

There are numerous awards for self-published children's books. The majority will charge a submission fee. The submission fee usually ranges from £50 to £200+ per title entered into each category. Some offer discounts if you enter more than one category. Also, look out for early bird discounts. If you enter far enough in advance of the closing date, it might give you a slightly discounted price. Some awards may require you to send them a physical copy of your book, while others will accept a digital version.

Displaying Your Winning Seal

Upon winning a book award, you will receive a winning seal that can be displayed on your book, website, and social media posts.

Chapter Summary

```
- Book awards honor exceptional literary works
across various genres.
- Winning or being nominated enhances an author's
reputation.
- Awards boost book visibility, potentially
increasing sales and readership.
- They validate an author's talent and add
credibility to their work.
- Awards offer valuable marketing opportunities.
- Numerous awards exist for self-published
children's books, with submission costs ranging from
£50 to £200+.
- Discounts may be available for multiple entries or
early submissions.
- Winners receive a seal for their book, website,
and social media.
```

24

Legal Deposit Regulations

Understanding Legal Deposit in the United Kingdom

In the United Kingdom, by law, you must send one copy of every publication (including e-books) to the British Library within one month of publication. The purpose of legal deposit is to ensure that a comprehensive collection of the nation's published output remains saved for future generations. The British Library is entitled to delivery free of charge.

Mailing Address for Legal Deposit

At the time of publishing this book, you need to send one copy of each of your publications to this postal address:
Legal Deposit Office

The British Library
Boston Spa
Wetherby
West Yorkshire
LS23 7BY

E-books can either be deposited by post or sent electronically.

The Five Main UK Libraries

Please note that you may receive an additional request to send five more copies of the book to be held by the other five main UK libraries.

You will need to send these copies *by post* to the address below:
Agency for the Legal Deposit Libraries
Unit 21 Marnin Way
Edinburgh
EH12 9GD

It is an option for you to send these five copies anyway without waiting for a formal request.

The five libraries involved in the operation of the Agency for the Legal Deposit Libraries are:

- Bodleian Libraries of the University of Oxford
- Cambridge University Library
- National Library of Scotland

- The Library of Trinity College Dublin, the University of Dublin
- National Library of Wales

These five libraries have the right to request materials from publishers under the legal deposit legislation. You can submit your work to them without waiting for them to request copies from you.

Automatic Right of the British Library

The British Library is a legal deposit library that has an automatic right to receive legal deposit materials.

Legal Deposit Benefits

The legal deposit system states the benefits as:

- Deposited publications are made available to users of the deposit libraries on their premises.
- Deposits are preserved for the benefit of future generations, and become part of the nation's heritage.
- Publications are recorded in online catalogues and become an essential research resource for generations to come.
- Books held in The British National Bibliography (BNB), are accessible by librarians and the book trade for stock

selection.
- Publishers have at times approached the deposit libraries for copies of their publications, which they no longer have but which have been preserved through legal deposit.
- Legal deposit supports a cycle of knowledge, whereby deposited works provide inspiration and source material for new books that will eventually achieve publication.

Chapter Summary

```
- Send one copy of every book format to the British
Library.
- This needs to be done within 1 month of
publication.
- You may receive a further request to send an
additional five copies to the Agency of Legal
Deposit Libraries, or you may choose to send these
copies to them.
```

25

Plush (Soft) Toys

Expanding Into Merchandise

Many authors consider expanding into merchandise, with plush toys often being a popular choice. I adore the combination of soft toys with books. Children love having the character in hand to act out the story. The set makes a perfect gift for book fans. Therefore, I delved into the possibility of transforming my book's characters into plush toys, starting with "Lucy Lamb's Most Curious Adventure".

While this endeavour required thorough investigation, I am delighted to share that Lucy Lamb and her brother have been successfully made into plush toys, which I couldn't be happier with. However, I must admit that the process of bringing these plush toys to life took longer than anticipated. In light of this, I am eager to share my journey with you, providing valuable insights to start you on your journey and to aid in your decision-making regarding whether to pursue plush toys.

Toy Safety Regulations

Initially, I started to investigate toy safety regulations. I started reading the latest regulations, specifically the Toy Safety Regulations 2011 of Great Britain.

I actively participated in toy safety social media groups. I sought advice, asked questions, and gained insights from fellow members. However, it's imperative to validate any information obtained to ensure its accuracy.

After carefully reviewing the regulations and engaging with toy safety social media groups, I determined that both the soft toy and the accompanying book fall under the regulations for toys intended for children under 14 years old. Consequently, they required testing to ensure compliance.

Seeking further validation, I contacted my local trading standards through the council. I was informed that since soft toys are popular with younger children, there was a likelihood that the toy could be purchased for a younger age group, so it was necessary for both the toy and the book to undergo chemical testing. Additionally, according to the regulations, any toy intended for children under 14 must undergo safety testing unless it falls under the exemption list, which neither the book nor the soft toy did. Moreover, as I intended to sell the soft toy alongside the picture book, they were considered a set, requiring both components to undergo testing.

Testing

On contacting a toy testing laboratory, I obtained the high-level costs. The lab went through the tests and sent me information.

The toy and book would need to be tested for:

- EN71-1: Mechanical and Physical: Various Tests
- EN71-2: Flammability
- EN71-3: Confirmation testing of chromium (VI)

Regulations are subject to change, so consider this information as a guide. A key takeaway is being aware that there are various tests required for compliance each with associated costs.

It's essential to conduct thorough research to ensure you have up-to-date and accurate information, as I did to validate the testing requirements.

For the book testing alone, I incurred a cost of just over £700. Additionally, there were costs associated with testing the soft toys. It's worth noting that the number of colours on the soft toy can impact the testing costs, as each colour requires separate testing. While you may not have control over the number of colours on your soft toy, it is something to consider due to its impact on testing costs.

As a rough estimate, the testing of the soft toys amounted to approximately £800.

Creating a Technical File

Once you have the test results, you need to create a technical file for the book and the soft toy. This took me a while to compile, as I could not find many examples or clear guidance on what needed to be documented. I consulted the testing laboratory, and the contact was super helpful. I spoke to trading standards again for further clarification.

The technical file needs to have a picture of the product and key information such as:

- Testing certification date.
- Item description.
- Item number.
- Age group it is intended for.
- Name of the manufacturer.
- Place of manufacture.
- Contact details for the manufacturer.
- Date of the test report.
- Report number.
- Document the testing results in a table.
- Keep the test results in the file.
- You also need to state any other information about the safety of the product and mitigation. For example, stating you will thoroughly check the toy over before dispatching,

storing it in an appropriate way, etc....

It's important to note that the requirements for a technical file may change, so I recommend researching to ensure you accurately compile your file and comply with the most up-to-date regulations. The testing laboratory may offer to create a technical file for you at an additional cost.

It's crucial to keep the file safe and accessible in case you need to produce it in the future to demonstrate compliance with the safety regulations.

Exploring Manufacturing Options

While delving into the toy safety regulations I concurrently explored manufacturing options for the soft toy. After thorough research I opted to reach out to a repeatedly recommended soft toy manufacturer in China known as GotaToy.

Upon providing pictures of Lucy and Harry from my book, the manufacturer promptly sent images of a sample soft toy. This allowed me to request any necessary changes to ensure they accurately produced the characters, and I was happy with the look.

Creating the Soft Toy Label

The other critical area to mention is the soft toy label. You must have the correct information on the label to comply with the regulations. I again researched this and spoke with trading standards. This is a mock-up of the final label I received from the manufacturer.

It is also important to mention that you must state an address on the label. I did not want to use my address, so I paid for a ghost mail address. Anything sent to the company that holds the ghost address will be sent to me. There is a small annual charge for this of just over £30.

Validate regulations at the start of your journey for the most up-to-date guidelines.

Requesting a Sample

I then proceeded to request a sample. My contact was super helpful, and it was an exceptionally smooth process.

When I received the soft toy samples of Lucy Lamb and her brother Harry, I was so happy with them that I was very keen to proceed.

As a guide, the samples and the postage were just over £100 (for two soft toy samples); however, costs can change for various reasons, so this is a guide only.

Once I had all the testing results from the book and the toy sample, I ordered the soft toys. Be aware of minimum order quantities. As a guide, I had to order three hundred of each toy. Consider where you are going to store them!

For 300 of each soft toy, the cost was just over £2000. The manufacturer arranged all the custom labels and delivered them to my door.

Reflecting on the Process

Reflecting on the summary it doesn't fully convey the extensive time and effort spent on research and discussions, along with the testing to complete to reach the stage of having the soft toy. It took nearly 12 months to receive my order of plush toys from start to finish. However, with the knowledge gained I anticipate that future endeavours in producing soft toys will be significantly faster. I'm confident that this insight will expedite your journey as well!

If you embark on creating a soft toy, I'd love to hear about your experience!

Chapter Summary

```
- Research the latest toy safety regulations
applicable to your location.
- Explore the costs associated with toy safety
testing.
- Identify potential manufacturers and obtain quotes.
- Familiarise yourself with label requirements for
plush toys.
- Ask for the minimum order quantities upfront.
- Calculate the overall expenses to anticipate costs.
```

- Consider storage options for the plush toys.
- Understand the documentation requirements for technical files and supporting information.

NOTE: This guide serves as a reference; ensure information is validated for your specific circumstances and regulations in your area at the time of starting your plush toy venture. Costs are subject to change, this is a guide only.

26

Traditional Publishing

As an author you will frequently be asked whether you have a publishing deal, or if you self-publish. This question often arises as one of the first asked. Ultimately, the choice is yours and it is essential to weigh the advantages and disadvantages of each option.

Traditionally, self-publishing was viewed with some scepticism, as it was often associated with lower-quality works. However, the market has significantly evolved and the perception of self-publishing has improved dramatically. Indie authors now enjoy a level of respect and legitimacy that was previously reserved for those with traditional publishing deals.

When you're asked if you have a publishing deal and you answer, "No, I chose to self-publish," say it proudly. Self-publishing is a significant achievement, reflecting your hard work, learning, and dedication. It's important to recognise that choosing to self-publish is a valid and respected path in the literary world today, and it should be celebrated as such.

I considered both options and I initially reached out to a select few publishing companies. This involved considerable time spent searching for publishers that were accepting submissions. Additionally, I made sure to target publishers open to receiving picture books.

My reason for considering a publishing deal was the many unknowns I faced about self-publishing and the concern that I would not have enough time to dedicate to achieving a book via the self-publishing route. Another unknown was how to market my book. The lack of knowledge about self-publishing when I began my journey as an author was one of the main drivers for writing this book. If I had known the information within this book back when I started, I would have felt more confident to consider self-publishing from the start and saved a lot of time.

Once I had identified several potential publishers, I customised my cover letter to align with their submission requirements, as these can vary significantly from one publisher to another. This tailored approach ensured my submissions were as targeted and effective as possible.

Submissions

It's worth noting that some publishers prefer to receive manuscripts as text-only submissions, while others accept fully illustrated books. Through my research, I discovered that the majority preferred text-only submissions.

The email application will usually request:

- Certain information to be displayed in the subject line. Usually consisting of:
- The author's name.
- Book title.
- Book genre.
- Publisher name you are contacting.
- A synopsis of the book in the main body.
- As picture books are not very long, usually you are requested to supply the whole story. Check what format they are requesting.
- You may be asked for examples of picture books that are similar to yours or why you feel your book will do well and stand out from others already published.
- Some publishers will ask for a brief background about you. An overview of the writing experience you have, and whether you have published anything else before.

Some publishers operate on a policy of only responding to successful submissions, while others provide feedback regardless of the outcome. The response times can vary widely, ranging from weeks to months.

Vanity Publishers

It's important to be aware of vanity publishers, a concept I wasn't familiar with when I began my publishing journey. When I started receiving offers and upon reading some, but not all, of the contract terms, they stated that the author was to pay a significant sum to the publishing company.

Further investigation revealed that these were vanity publishers. Unlike traditional publishers who cover the costs of editing, design, printing, and distribution, vanity publishers require authors to foot the bill for these services. As a result, their selection process may be less rigorous, and they may accept a wide range of manuscripts.

It's crucial to recognise that vanity publishers may offer limited distribution compared to traditional publishing avenues. Despite paying a significant sum, your book may not reach as many outlets or receive the marketing efforts you'd expect.

If you're presented with an offer from a publisher requiring you to pay for services, it's essential to conduct thorough research. Understand the costs involved, the quality of services provided, and the potential benefits and limitations of such a deal beyond simply seeing your book in print.

I chose to decline offers where I was requested to pay a large sum of money to the publisher. If you are being asked to pay a publisher for the services they should provide, this seems the wrong way round!

Self-publishing Stigma

So, whilst I did reach out to publishing companies and carefully considered their offers, I ultimately chose to decline and threw myself wholeheartedly into the self-publishing journey. I have thoroughly enjoyed this process and feel proud that my determination and perseverance have gotten me to where I am today.

You may encounter some lingering stigma about self-publishing versus gaining a traditional publishing contract. However, if you encounter this, brush it off, as it is becoming a dated view. Hold your head high, as becoming a self-published author, also known as an indie author, offers numerous benefits.

Self-publishing Benefits

Firstly, you will have full control over the publishing process. You will decide who illustrates your book, determine the cost, and choose where to upload it for sale. On the flip side this will require an investment from your pocket. However, you remain in control of the budget and can consider this when selecting an illustrator. Illustration costs vary widely based on experience and location. With diligent research you can find an illustrator who can deliver the desired style within your budget. You just need to search for them. You might, however, have the skills to illustrate yourself or the desire to learn, which in the long run will save you this cost completely.

Secondly, the distribution channel of traditional publishers is seen as an advantage. However, due to the vast amount of books being published you would need to ensure that your book is on the shelf and can be seen against many others. Going the self-published route allows you to reach out to book stores and outlets directly to sell your book. This may take a little bit of time, but with determination and persistence, it is possible to have your book accepted. If so, you will receive more income for your book when selling directly.

Thirdly, it is often assumed that traditional publishing contracts cover all the marketing costs for your book. In reality this may not always be the case. The publishing company may still request that you cover part or all of the costs yourself. Self-publishing grants you control over your marketing and its associated costs. While it may seem daunting at first you will gradually learn marketing strategies and be able to target your niche market. It also can be fun designing your marketing content and your creative juices will be even more satisfied!

The last point to add would be about how much you will make per book sale, known as royalties. When you upload your book to selling platforms they will deduct a fee per sale. This fee is usually much less than what a traditional publishing company would retain. On average for a printed paperback book (though this can vary based on several factors) you would make approximately 10% per book sale with a traditional publishing company. With self-publishing you could make as much as 25% per book sale. Factors influencing this percentage include the number of pages your book has, the trim size (size of your book), and sometimes the option to select print quality.

There are various tools online to assist you with calculating what royalty you will receive. Here is one I have used before through Kindlepreneur:

KDP Royalty Calculator: Free Tool for Authors (kindlepreneur.com)

In the future would I consider a traditional publishing deal? Of course, however, the terms would have to be right for me. For now I am perfectly fine with self-publishing and continuing my journey while controlling every aspect.

My ultimate goal is to continue making my biggest inspiration, my daughter, proud of me. Seeing a big smile on her face when she sees my books in outlets, when I visit her school for book readings and presentations, and when I launch a new book is more than enough for me. Everything else I am extremely grateful for, however this gives me the most pleasure.

Chapter Summary

- If you would like to reach out to publishing companies, take your time to select the ones open for manuscripts suitable for your book.
- Tailor the application to the publisher's requirements.
- Supply the book text in the right format and add the copyright symbol to your work.
- Make a note of the response timelines; once passed, if you do not hear, assume you will not hear back.
- Be aware of vanity publishers.
- Do not dwell on how you achieved your published book, having the finished book in your hand what you created is the goal.

27

Glossary of Terms

Book Proof - A book proof is a pre-publication copy of a book that is used for final review and correction before the book is officially printed and distributed. It allows authors, editors, and publishers to check for errors in text, layout, formatting, and design, ensuring that the final version of the book is polished and error-free.

Copyright - Copyright is a legal protection granted to creators of original works, including books, to control the use and distribution of their work. It gives authors exclusive rights to reproduce, distribute, perform, display, and adapt their creations. This protection encourages creativity by ensuring that creators can benefit from their work and prevent others from using it without permission. Copyright is automatically granted to authors upon creation of their work, but registration with relevant authorities can provide additional legal benefits and protections.

Edition - An edition refers to a specific version or iteration of a book that has been published at a particular time. It may include updates, revisions, or modifications from previous editions, and can vary in content, layout, design, or format. Editions are often distinguished by edition numbers (e.g., first edition, second edition) and may indicate significant changes or improvements made to the book. Multiple editions of a book can exist over time, reflecting the evolution of the work or the needs of readers and markets.

EPUB Files - EPUB files are a standard format for digital books, offering compatibility with e-readers and software platforms. They include text, images, and formatting for a user-friendly reading experience.

First Edition - The first print run of a book.

ISBN - ISBN, or International Standard Book Number, is a unique identifier assigned to books and other monographic publications. It helps to identify a specific edition of a book and is used for cataloguing, ordering, and inventory management purposes. ISBNs typically consist of 13 digits (formerly 10), including a prefix indicating the country or language group, followed by a publisher code, title code, and a check digit. They are essential for tracking and managing books throughout the publishing and distribution process.

Manuscript - A manuscript refers to the original draft or copy of a written work before it is published. It can include handwritten or typed pages, digital documents, or any other form of text that serves as the basis for a book, article, or other publication. Manuscripts may undergo multiple revisions and edits before being finalised for publication, and they often contain annotations, comments, and corrections made by authors or editors during the writing process.

Metadata - Metadata refers to data that describes the book content to aid online discoverability. This is typically the title, author, ISBN, key terms, description and other bibliographic information.

Page Proofs - Page proofs, also known as galley proofs or printer's proofs, are the preliminary versions of a publication that are printed for final review and correction before the work is officially printed and distributed. Page proofs are typically generated from the final manuscript and formatted to resemble the layout of the finished product, including pagination, fonts, and illustrations. Authors, editors, and proofreaders carefully examine page proofs to identify and correct errors in text, layout, or formatting before the publication goes to press. Once any necessary revisions have been made and approved, the final version is prepared for printing and publication.

PDF - PDF, short for Portable Document Format, is a widely used file format developed by Adobe that preserves the layout and formatting of documents regardless of the software, hardware, or operating system used to view or print them.

Print on Demand (POD) - Print on demand (POD) is a publishing model where books are printed as they are ordered, rather than being printed in large quantities upfront. This allows for efficient and cost-effective production, as books are only printed when there is demand for them. POD eliminates the need for publishers to invest in large print runs and warehouse storage, reducing the risk of overstocking and minimising upfront costs. Additionally, POD enables authors to self-publish their works with minimal investment, since they can print small quantities or even single copies of their books as needed. This model has revolutionised the publishing industry by making it easier for authors to get their works into print and reach readers worldwide.

Royalty - For self-publishers, book royalties refer to the portion of revenue earned from book sales that the author retains after deducting any production, distribution, and retailer costs. Unlike traditional publishing where authors receive advances and royalties from a publishing house, self-published authors retain full control over their work but also bear the responsibility for all aspects of publishing, including editing, design, distribution, and marketing. Self-publishing platforms typically offer different royalty models, often based on factors such as the book's format, pricing, and distribution channels. Authors may receive royalties as a percentage of the book's list price or net sales revenue. While self-publishing provides authors with higher royalty rates compared to traditional publishing, they also incur the upfront costs of publishing and may need to invest in marketing efforts to drive book sales. Overall, self-publishing royalties represent the earnings authors receive directly from the sales of their books, reflecting their independence and ownership of the publishing process.

Trade Discount - Trade discounts for self-publishers refer to the discount offered to retailers or distributors when they purchase copies of the book for resale. As a self-publisher, you may offer trade discounts to encourage retailers to carry your book in their stores or list it in their catalogues. The trade discount is typically a percentage of the book's list price and can vary depending on factors such as the distribution channel, the retailer's policies, and the author's goals. Offering a competitive trade discount can help attract more retailers to stock your book, potentially increasing its visibility and sales. However, it's essential to strike a balance between offering an attractive trade discount and ensuring that you still earn a profit from each sale. Negotiating trade discounts requires careful consideration of your production costs, distribution expenses, and overall sales strategy.

Trim Size - Trim size refers to the final dimensions of a printed book after it has been trimmed along the edges. It is typically measured in inches or millimetres and represents the width and height of the book's pages. Choosing the right trim size is an important decision for authors and publishers as it can impact the book's appearance, readability, and production costs. Authors and publishers should carefully consider the implications of trim size selection on factors like layout, design, printing costs, and shelf space utilization when determining the best option for their book.

28

Useful information

There is a lot of resources available to you when you have a search. Here are a few of mine that I have found useful.

Advocate Art
https://www.advocate-art.com
Advocate Art represents leading illustrators who produce children's and decorative work to commission of license. You will find a lot of chose to search through thumbs nails of work to decide on styles.

Amazon Author
Amazon Author
https://author.amazon.com/

Amazon.co.uk: Trudy Davidson: books, biography, latest update
https://www.amazon.co.uk/stores/Trudy-Davidson/author/B09X73W5GM

Dictionary
https://www.dictionary.com/

FIVERR
Fiverr - Freelance Services Marketplace
https://www.fiverr.com/

Fiverr is an online marketplace that connects freelancers with clients who need digital services. I have hired from here before.

Freelancer
Hire Freelancers & Find Freelance Jobs Online | Freelancer
https://www.freelancer.com/

Go Daddy
https://www.godaddy.com/en-uk
GoDaddy offers a number of web services for individuals, as well as small and large businesses. From its most popular services, such as domain registration and web hosting to niche services

Google Drive
https://www.google.com/drive/
File sharing platform that provides a personal, secure cloud storage option to share content with other users.

Gotatoy
Soft toy manufacturer based in China.
Gotatoy@126.com
www.igotatoy.com

Gov.UK Copyright
Intellectual property: Copyright - GOV.UK (www.gov.uk)
https://www.gov.uk/government/organisations/intellectual-property-office

Guru
Guru.com - Find and Hire Expert Freelancers
https://www.guru.com/

Kindlepreneur
Kindlepreneur - Book Marketing for Self-Publishing Authors
https://kindlepreneur.com/

Free marketing resource

Kindlepreneur
https://kindlepreneur.com/present-tense/

Writing in present tense

Kindlepreneur
https://kindlepreneur.com/past-tense/

Writing in past tense

Metricool
https://metricool.com/
A social media management and analytics platform that provides tools for scheduling posts, analysing performance, and monitoring metrics across various social media platforms.

It offers features such as content scheduling, audience engagement tracking, hashtag analysis, and detailed analytics reports.

Mind Mapping
https://xmind.app/
Xmind is a tool that can be used to generate visual diagrams and mind maps. It is a document file type that contains multiple sheets with diagrams that capture ideas during a brainstorming session.

Nielson's Barcodes
Nielsen UK ISBN Store (nielsenisbnstore.com)
https://www.nielsenisbnstore.com/Home/Barcodes

Barcode store

Neilsons Book Data UK
Nielsenbook-UK
https://nielsenbook.co.uk/

Nielsen BookData provides a range of services to the book industry internationally, aiding the discovery and purchase, distribution and sales measurement of books. They run the ISBN and SAN Agencies for UK & Ireland and offer publishers a range of services from assigning an ISBN to your book to adding your metadata to our database and promotional tools to help market your book.

Nielson's ISBNs
Nielsen UK ISBN Store (nielsenisbnstore.com)
https://www.nielsenisbnstore.com/Home/Isbn

ISBN Store

Publisher Compensation - Ingram Sparks

myaccount.ingramspark.com/Portal/Tools/PubCompCalculator
https://myaccount.ingramspark.com/Portal/Tools/PubCompCalculator

To calculate print costs.

Publisher Rocket
Publisher Rocket | Optimize Your Book's Amazon Success
https://publisherrocket.com/?affiliate=tdavidson

A software tool designed for authors and publishers, particularly those that have self-published. It focuses on trying to help optimize marketing efforts on selling platforms. It covers areas such as keywords, category searches and competitor analysis to name a few. It is a one-off fee for life at the moment with unlimited use.

Reedsy
Exports - Your Ultimate Guide To Writing Picture Books And Self Publishing - Reedsy
https://reedsy.com/hire/us/developmental-editors/

Reedsy is an online author service marketplace that provides book production services to authors in the self-publishing industry. It has a variety of freelancers available for hire, specifically in book editing, design, ghostwriting, and more.

Reedsy is more than just a book formatting tool, it provides a number of services to help authors polish up their works.

Rhyme Zone
https://www.rhymezone.com/
Find rhymes, synonyms, adjectives, and more!

Slide Share

Share & Discover Presentations | SlideShare
https://www.slideshare.net/

Online platform for sharing presentations, infographics, documents, and professional videos

Society of Children's Book Writers and Illustrators - SCBWI
https://www.scbwi.org
SCBWI is an organisation for children's book creators. They are a community of writers, illustrators, translators, publishers, librarians, and other industry professionals related to children's literature. It has worldwide members.

You can either do the free sneak peek account or choose one of the memberships, which has a fee attached to it.

Survey Monkey
SurveyMonkey: The World's Most Popular Free Online Survey Tool
https://www.surveymonkey.com/

The Society of Authors
https://www2.societyofauthors.org/about-us/

UK's largest trade union for all types of writers. There are some free guides to download and if you choose to become a member there is unlimited free advice on all aspects of the profession.

Thesaurus
https://www.thesaurus.com/

WeTransfer
https://wetransfer.com/
A great tool to send large files and pictures

Free online survey tool

Writers Helping Writers
https://www.writershelpingwriters.co.uk
A website full of many tools and resources. You can also join webinars and workshops on various topics.

Writers and Artists Yearbook
A very large book packed with advice and guidance for authors and illustrators.

I am not affiliated with any of these, apart from Publisher Rocket where I receive a small fee if you sign up using the link I have provided, it is just to provide you with some of the resources and tools I have used along the way that I feel you may also find useful.

Epilogue

You've reached the end of this guide, based on my own experience and the knowledge I would have liked to have been able to read in one place at the start of my journey.

Now, it's time for you to take this knowledge and expand upon it. Remember, the journey of writing and self-publishing is a continuous learning process with endless opportunities for growth and improvement.

There may be moments when you feel discouraged, due to writer's block, modest book sales, modest compensation, or the sheer number of authors in the industry. However, always remember why you started on this journey in the first place, the achievements you've already made, and the passion you have for writing. Don't give up; keep pushing forward!

Remind yourself why you started your writing journey and where the idea for the book came from. I'm sure these two questions alone will keep you moving forward.

Focus on your journey and avoid comparing yourself to others. Each person's path is unique, and yours is no exception. Embrace the experience of sharing and learning from others, and take pride that every book sold means someone is enjoying your work.

Don't hesitate to celebrate your accomplishments along the way. Promote them proudly and continue to market your work with enthusiasm. Above all, enjoy every moment of this journey.

Enjoy the process, relish your achievements, and continue your passion for writing.

```
It would mean the world if you could take a few
minutes to leave a short review on Amazon. Feedback
is so important to authors, which you will soon
discover. Thanks so much in advance for your time.
```

I wish you every success with your writing. – Good luck.

Trudy

www.ingramcontent.com/pod-product-compliance
Lightning Source LLC
Chambersburg PA
CBHW051538020426
42333CB00016B/1997